STAY YOUR BLADE FROM THE
FLESH OF AN INNOCENT

HIDE IN PLAIN SIGHT

NEVER COMPROMISE
THE BROTHERHOOD

ASSASSIN'S CREED

An Hachette UK Company
www.hachette.co.uk

First published in Great Britain in 2018 by
ILEX, a division of Octopus Publishing Group Ltd
Octopus Publishing Group
Carmelite House
50 Victoria Embankment
London, EC4Y 0DZ
www.octopusbooks.co.uk

Originally published in France in 2017 by
Hachette Heroes, a division of Hachette Pratique (Hachette Livre)
58 rue, Jean Bleuzen, 92178 Vanves Cedex

Distributed in the U.S. by
Hachette Book Group
1290 Avenue of the Americas
4th and 5th Floors
New York, NY 10104

Distributed in Canada by
Canadian Manda Group
664 Annette St.
Toronto, Ontario, Canada M6S 2C8

Hachette Livre
Content Director: Catherine Saunier-Talec
Project Director: Antoine Béon
Project Manager: Jean-Baptiste Roux
Design and layout: Mélody Denturck
Production: Amélie Latsch

Ilex
Licensing Director: Roly Allen
Publishing Assistant: Stephanie Hetherington
Art Director: Julie Weir
Managing Editor: Frank Gallaugher
Translation from French: Alison Murray, in association
with First Edition Translations Ltd, Cambridge, UK

ISBN 978-1-78157-630-4

A CIP catalogue record for this book is available from the British Library

Printed and bound in China

10 9 8 7 6 5 4 3 2 1

GUILLAUME DELALANDE

ILLUSTRATIONS BY **BUNKA**

ASSASSIN'S
—CREED—
INFOGRAPHICS

ilex

INTRODUCTION:
WE WORK IN THE DARK
TO SERVE THE LIGHT

In just over ten years, with more than 100 million copies sold around the world, *Assassin's Creed* has become a hugely popular video game franchise. It is also available in a number of other media: novels, movies, comics, an animated series in the works—and the universe of the game has been enriched and deepened with each new release.

Since 2007 and the escapades of Altaïr in the Third Crusade, followed by further adventures in the golden age of piracy in the Caribbean, the American and French Revolutions, and Renaissance Italy, to name a few, a complex mythology has been created. Dozens of stories intersect and feed back into one another, creating a global and transmedia environment. At times, this can seem overwhelming to beginners, owing to its complexity. The aim of *Assassin's Creed Infographics* is to give you the keys to understanding all the different components of this universe.

There's something for everyone in *Assassin's Creed*. Heart-stopping adventures at the most epic moments of history, science fiction showing us that humankind is the creation of an ancient civilization, secret societies that battle in the shadows and occasionally in broad daylight, and philosophies with opposing views on the very foundations of our humanity. *Assassin's Creed* encompasses all of this.

Assassin's Creed Infographics offers a global approach to the saga through the innovative lens of information panels, diagrams, and, above all, the superb illustrations of Bunka. It's impossible for us to cover absolutely everything here. Instead, our primary aim is one of discovery and rediscovery by exploring information carefully collected from the games and other works. It's the perfect little revision manual before getting back to your controller!

Guillaume Delalande

 CONTENTS

CHAPTER 1
THE ASSASSIN'S CREED UNIVERSE

IN THE BEGINNING . . .

The origins of the opposition between Assassins and Templars can be found in the dramatic events that marked the early years of the human race, and in particular the war fought against its creators, the Isu.

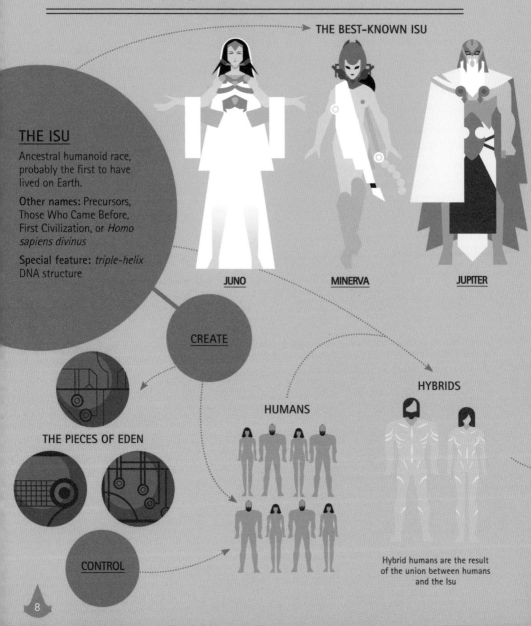

THE BEST-KNOWN ISU

THE ISU

Ancestral humanoid race, probably the first to have lived on Earth.

Other names: Precursors, Those Who Came Before, First Civilization, or *Homo sapiens divinus*

Special feature: *triple-helix* DNA structure

JUNO

MINERVA

JUPITER

CREATE

THE PIECES OF EDEN

HUMANS

HYBRIDS

CONTROL

Hybrid humans are the result of the union between humans and the Isu

TEMPLARS
Guide humankind to
enlightened perfection

ASSASSINS
Liberate humankind from all control

BIRTH OF TWO PHILOSOPHIES
Two opposing philosophies emerge over the use of artifacts: they
represent the ideologies of the future Assassins and Templars.

Humans and surviving Isu help each other to rebuild the planet,
but the Isu eventually die out. They leave behind a large number
of artifacts that can be used to control non-hybrid humans.

Thanks to her calculations,
Minerva understands that
another catastrophe will
take place in 2012 and that
only one individual, known
as Desmond, can stop it.

Minerva creates vaults
where she stores messages
for Desmond so that he
can save the planet from
a new disaster.

TOBA CATASTROPHE
The Earth is struck by a solar flare.
Only 10,000 humans and a few Isu survive.

Increase in the
number of hybrid
humans over
whom the Pieces
of Eden have little
controlling effect.

75,010 BCE
Human–Isu War led by Adam and Eve, two hybrid humans. The war lasts
ten years. The war distracts humans and the Isu from noticing that a massive
solar flare is heading toward the Earth, threatening to destroy everything.

THE PIECES
OF EDEN

The Isu kept total control over humanity with a series of specially designed artifacts. Other creations had a more specific goal. In the modern era, humans have sometimes been able to use the powers of these artifacts for purely personal ends.

KOH-I-NOOR

105,602-carat diamond.

Powers: Creation of illusions and interference with the powers of all artifacts. This artifact can be controlled only by an Isu or by women with high levels of Isu DNA. Men with high levels of Isu DNA are able to control it, but only for short periods and at great risk to themselves.

Number of known pieces: 1

SHROUDS

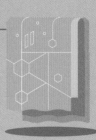

Invented by the Isu scientist Consus in 75,383 BCE (1923 of the Isu Era).

Powers: Healing of all wounds. Consus also transferred his own consciousness to the Shrouds, allowing him to take control of certain users.

Number of known pieces: 2

ANKH OF EDEN

Rumors speak of an Ankh of Eden, with the power to heal the sick and temporarily resurrect the dead. The existence of the artifact appears to be a hoax perpetuated by the Assassins to fool the Templars.

Existence and location of this artifact are unknown.

APPLES OF EDEN

Originally created to enslave humanity.

Powers: Creation of illusions and mental manipulation. They can be used to predict complex probabilities about the future. They also contain information on the First Civilization and can be used as communication devices.

Wielded by Adam and Eve and numerous world leaders (sometimes when camouflaged as an imperial orb), for example by Elizabeth I of England, Napoleon Bonaparte, George Washington, and Adolf Hitler.

Number of known pieces: 8

CRYSTAL BALLS

Powers: Communication with the Nexus zone and the Isu spirits resident there.

Number of known pieces: 2

SWORDS OF EDEN

Created by the Isu scientist Hephaestus.

Powers: Charisma and negation of the effects of other illusions. If activated by a Heart sphere or worn by a hybrid with Isu DNA, it can project energy blasts and allow instant translocation.

Wielded most notably by King Arthur, Attila the Hun, Joan of Arc, and Genghis Khan.

Number of known pieces: 2

SHARDS OF EDEN

Powers: Projection of an electromagnetic field that protects their wearers, allowing deflection of bullets.

Number of known pieces: 1

CRYSTAL SKULLS

There are three types.

Powers: Communication between two individuals possessing a Crystal Skull (type I); recording and playback (type II); monitoring (type III).

Mainly found in South and Central America.

Number of known pieces: at least 3

MEMORY SEALS

Created to record brief memories. Five of the seals were also used as keys to open the library of Altaïr in the fortress of Masyaf.

Number of known pieces: 9

STAVES OF EDEN

Certain staves are known as the Papal Staff, Russian Imperial Scepter, and Piece of Eden 34

Powers: Human mind control, creation of doubles, levitation, and invisibility.

Wielded by numerous pharaohs; by Moses to create the illusion of parting the Red Sea; John the Baptist; Alexander the Great in the creation of his empire; and Tsar Alexander III.

Number of known pieces: 3

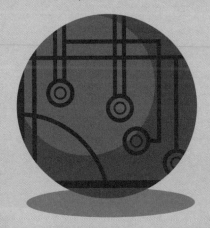

APPLES OF EDEN

APPLE 1

Taken by Arno Dorian from the Saint-Denis Temple in northern Paris. Napoleon acquires it and becomes Emperor of the French thanks to its power. The Apple passes into the hands of the magician Harry Houdini. The Templars eliminate him and take the Apple back.

Known owners: Suger of Saint-Denis, Arno Dorian, Napoleon, and Harry Houdini

Uses: By Napoleon to become emperor; assassination of John F. Kennedy

Current status: In the hands of the Templars

Appearances: AC Unity

APPLE 3

Brought by European Freemasons to the New World where it comes into the possession of George Washington. Haunted by dreams of totalitarian tyranny made possible by the Apple, he gives it to Ratonhnhaké:ton (Connor) so he can throw it into the sea. Franklin D. Roosevelt recovers it and passes it down to his successors until it reaches John F. Kennedy, who will be assassinated by the Templars.

Known owners: George Washington, Ratonhnhaké:ton (Connor), Franklin D. Roosevelt, and John F. Kennedy

Uses: Progression of the Apollo 11 project and retrieval of the Fifth Apple from the Moon

Current status: Unknown, probably in the hands of the Templars

Appearances: AC III

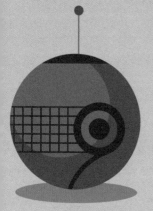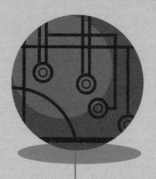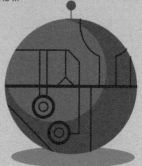

APPLE 2

Apple of Eden reactivated by Bayek. Used in conjunction with the Staff of Eden of Alexander the Great, it opens the Temple of Amun in Siwa.

Owned by Al Mualim, the old Sage and Mentor of the Assassins of Masyaf. Altaïr exposes him as a traitor and takes possession of it. In the 16th century, it falls into the hands of Elizabeth I of England. It is later owned by Gandhi.

Known owners: Bayek, Al Mualim, Altaïr, Elizabeth I, and Gandhi

Current status: Destroyed in an accident at Denver International Airport (2011)

Appearances: AC, AC Revelations, AC Origins

The Isu created dozens of Apples to control humanity. Their powers and ease of use make them priority artifacts for Assassins and Templars.

APPLE 5

Sent into space by Jupiter, Juno, and Minerva, and crashed into the Moon. It is recovered from the Moon by NASA on 20th July 1969 during the Apollo 11 mission.

Known owners: First Civilization and NASA

Current status: Probably in the hands of NASA

Appearances: AC II

APPLE 7

Destroyed on February 10, 1868 by David Brewster during an experiment in his laboratory in Croydon.

Appearances: AC Syndicate

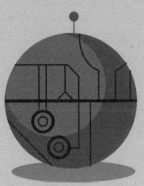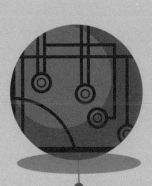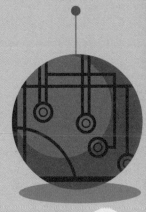

APPLE 4

The earliest known depiction dates back to 10th-century China. The first known owner is Nikola Tesla who wants to use its energy to create free electricity for the entire world. The Templar Thomas Edison gains possession of it. It then falls into the hands of Mark Twain, followed by Henry Ford, who uses it to create mass-production assembly lines, ensuring the triumph of Capitalism. Following the instructions of the Templars, he then sends the Apple to Adolf Hitler so that he can take power in Germany and start a world war favorable to Templar industry.

Known owners: Nikola Tesla, Thomas Edison, Henry Ford and Adolf Hitler

Uses: Inspires the Chinese to invent gunpowder and the first firearms; assists with the creation of the Tesla coil; creation of a Hitler double

Current status: Unknown, probably owned by the Assassins

Appearances: AC

APPLE 6

Also known as Ezio's Apple of Eden.

Known owners: Sultan Mehmet II, Rodrigo Borgia, Ezio Auditore, Caterina Sforza, Girolamo Savonarola, Mario Auditore, Cesare Borgia, Leonardo da Vinci, and Desmond Miles

Current status: in the possession of William Miles

Appearances: AC II, AC Brotherhood, AC Revelations, AC III

EZIO'S APPLE

OTHER

1453
CONSTANTINOPLE
Sultan Mehmet II uses the Apple
to conquer Constantinople.

1482
CYPRUS
Cem, son of Sultan Mehmet II,
hides the Apple in Cyprus.

1486
VENICE
The Apple is brought back from Cyprus
by the Templars (led by Rodrigo Borgia),
then retaken by Ezio.

1488
FORLÌ
Ezio sets out to hide the Apple in the
fortress of Ravaldino in Forlì.

OF EDEN

1498
FLORENCE

Girolamo Savonarola uses the Apple to subject Florence to his religious dictatorship.

It is sometimes difficult to follow the trail of the dozens of artifacts scattered around the planet. The travels of Ezio's Apple of Eden are a central feature of *Assassin's Creed II* and *Assassin's Creed Brotherhood*.

1499
ROME – VATICAN

Confrontation between Ezio and Rodrigo Borgia. During the battle, Rodrigo retrieves the Apple of Eden, which, used with the Papal Staff, opens the vault.

JAN 1500
MONTERIGGIONI

Cesare Borgia lays siege to the Villa Auditore and retakes the Apple.

1501
ROME

Leonardo da Vinci is forced to study the Apple in order to create war machines for Cesare Borgia.

1501
ROME

Following the death of Rodrigo Borgia, Ezio recaptures the Apple and then uses it to defeat the forces of Cesare Borgia. After this victory, Ezio uses the Apple while in the company of Leonardo. It reveals the escape of Cesare.

1504
ROME

Ezio uses the Apple with Niccolò Machiavelli to find Micheletto Corella. After this, the two men hide it in the vault under the Colosseum.

2012
NEW YORK

Desmond retrieves the Apple hidden by Ezio in the Colosseum Vault. The Apple is used to open the Grand Temple. It has most likely been in the possession of William Miles since then.

1499
MONTERIGGIONI

The Assassins study the Apple.

1499
ROME – VATICAN

Mario Auditore takes the Apple from the hands of the Borgia and promises to protect it in Monteriggioni.

15

CHAPTER 2
ASSASSINS
VS
TEMPLARS

ASSASSINS

V

"WE WORK IN THE DARK TO SERVE THE LIGHT"

We need to go beyond the illusion of the world and find the wisdom in it while accepting that we are responsible for our lives and all the consequences of our choices.

Rebellion of Humans against the Isu using the Apple of Eden taken by Adam and Eve, two hybrids over whom the artifact had less effect.

75000 BCE

Bayek and Aya found the "Hidden Ones," an organization with an ideology similar to that of the Assassins. Aya takes part in the assassination of Julius Caesar.

49 BCE

YEAR 0

The Brotherhood becomes a public organization operating out of the fortress of Masyaf, and the Assassins take part in the Crusades. Altaïr eliminates Grand Master Robert de Sablé.

1191

Marco Polo dies, assassinated by the Templars. Before his death he secures Altaïr's Codex and bequeathes his fortune to Domenico Auditore, who settles in Florence. Domenico will be the patriarch of a large family of Assassins that will spread the Creed throughout Europe.

1324

During the American Revolution, Ratonhnhaké:ton (Connor) reduces the Templar presence in the American colonies to almost nothing.

1775–1783

The Brotherhood doctrine shifts toward the peaceful political change taking place within political regimes. The Assassin Brotherhood acquires the support of a hacking collective known as Erudito. Only a few Assassin cells are left in the world.

20ᵀᴴ CENTURY

CURRENT ORGANIZATION

A handful of Assassin cells are still operational in the world. William Miles is their leader, but all cells have acted independently of one another ever since the Templars began hunting them down.

S TEMPLARS ✷

"MAY THE FATHER OF UNDERSTANDING GUIDE US"

This maxim, which is still used today, does not so much refer to an actual divine entity, but rather to the vision of the role of the Templars as shepherds of humanity. Some believe that the Father of Understanding is a reference to Grand Master Jacques de Molay, who died as a martyr for the Templar Order.

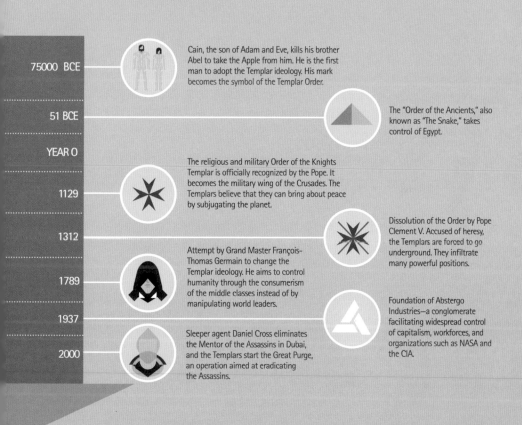

75000 BCE — Cain, the son of Adam and Eve, kills his brother Abel to take the Apple from him. He is the first man to adopt the Templar ideology. His mark becomes the symbol of the Templar Order.

51 BCE — The "Order of the Ancients," also known as "The Snake," takes control of Egypt.

YEAR 0

1129 — The religious and military Order of the Knights Templar is officially recognized by the Pope. It becomes the military wing of the Crusades. The Templars believe that they can bring about peace by subjugating the planet.

1312 — Dissolution of the Order by Pope Clement V. Accused of heresy, the Templars are forced to go underground. They infiltrate many powerful positions.

1789 — Attempt by Grand Master François-Thomas Germain to change the Templar ideology. He aims to control humanity through the consumerism of the middle classes instead of by manipulating world leaders.

1937 — Foundation of Abstergo Industries—a conglomerate facilitating widespread control of capitalism, workforces, and organizations such as NASA and the CIA.

2000 — Sleeper agent Daniel Cross eliminates the Mentor of the Assassins in Dubai, and the Templars start the Great Purge, an operation aimed at eradicating the Assassins.

CURRENT ORGANIZATION

The Inner Sanctum is one of the highest governmental bodies of the Templar Order. It is responsible for the supervision of Grand Masters around the world. The Inner Sanctum reports only to the mysterious General of the Cross.

Abstergo
Industries

Foundation: 1937 by Henry Ford with President Roosevelt's blessing.

Purpose: order and discipline through power and global control.

Operating budget: estimated at three billion dollars (2016), funded entirely by the Templars.

Influence: Controls the IMF, World Bank, NASA, the CIA, and most international corporations.

ⓧ SUBSIDIARIES

- Abstergo Pharmaceuticals
- Abstergo Fitness
- Abstergo Entertainment (creator of video games including *Liberation*), headquartered in Montreal
- Abstergo Financial Group & Malta Banking Corporation
- Abstergo Foundation (in Madrid)
- Abstergo Medical (clinics used to scan the DNA of people seeking care)
- MysoreTech (Indian subsidiary in charge of the Brahman VR)
- Historical Research
- Lineage Discovery and Acquisition (location and abduction of Assassins and their descendants)

ⓧ PRODUCTS

PHARMACEUTICAL
Most medicines in the world come from Abstergo laboratories. They are sometimes experimental, such as the food supplement Herne+ which makes the population more sensitive to the Apples of Eden.

ENTERTAINMENT
Video game system in the Helix cloud: historical propaganda glorifying the Templars and recovery of DNA data from users through Brahman VR headsets.

FITNESS
The Angelus baby monitor is used to control the hormones and brain function of newborns. Bodyband, the version for adults, can also be used to geolocate individuals.

The public face of the Templars since 1937, Abstergo Industries uses its influence to control numerous institutions and industrial corporations. Some of its activities also revolve around scientific research and artifact acquisition. Only its leaders are aware of the links with the Templars, when they are not leading dignitaries of the Order themselves.

⊗ PROGRAMS

ANIMUS PROJECT

Program launched in 1980 by Dr Warren Vidic.

Objective: To create a device that can read the genetic memories contained in the DNA of Assassins and their descendants in order to locate the Pieces of Eden. Until the creation of Helix technology, the subject had to be inside the machine to decode memories.

Project status: Public

PROJECT LEGACY

Objective: To analyze the genetic memories of certain individuals not necessarily connected with the Assassins. The project used the DDS (Data Dump Scanner) software of the Animus. The project was put on hold in 2012 following the actions of hackers from the Erudito collective.

Project status: Secret

ANIMI TRAINING PROGRAM

Objective: To allow Abstergo employees to acquire combat skills by reliving the memories of Assassins through transposition.

Project status: Secret

ARCHEOLOGY

Objective: To research the locations and artifacts of the First Civilization.

EYE-ABSTERGO

Objective: To deploy a satellite system to control the population through an Apple of Eden placed in orbit. The Apple was scheduled for launch on 21st December 2012. Project abandoned in 2012.

Project status: Secret

⊗ ABSTERGO FACILITIES

Abstergo Industries has a global presence with offices in:

Paris	Tokyo
Rome	Seoul
Madrid	Osaka-Kobe
London	Shanghai
New York	Moscow
Chicago	Philadelphia
Los Angeles	

Animus

A central component of Abstergo Industries technology, this is a virtual reality machine that projects the genetic memories of the user in 3D. There is one condition, however: that the user stay in perfect synchronization with the historical subject.

ANIMUS 1.0

Developer: Abstergo Industries
Launch date: 1980
Properties: The procedure is recorded as being extremely dangerous and painful.
Known users: Subject 1 and Warren Vidic (Subject 2)
Release: Limited to Abstergo

ANIMUS 1.09

Developer: Abstergo Industries
Launch date: 1980
Known user: Daniel Cross (Subject 4)
Release: Limited to Abstergo Industries

ANIMUS VR

Developer: Abstergo Entertainment
Launch date: 2014–15
Presence of subject analyzed: Unnecessary
Properties: This is the version of the Brahman VR developed for the North American market. Available in different versions and for all budgets, it is a commercial success.
Known user: Charlotte de la Cruz
Release: General public, North American market

ANIMUS 1.28

Developer: Abstergo Industries
Launch date: 2002
Presence of subject analyzed: Mandatory
Risk of Bleeding Effect: Low
Known users: Daniel Cross (Subject 4), Clay Kaczmarek (Subject 16), and Desmond Miles (Subject 17)
Release: Limited to Abstergo Industries

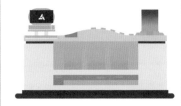

ANIMUS 2.0

Developer: Assassin Brotherhood, under the direction of Rebecca Crane
Launch date: 2012
Presence of subject analyzed: Mandatory
Risk of Bleeding Effect: Moderate
Properties: The Animus is developed with the assistance of Lucy Stillman, an Assassin spy at Abstergo.
Known user: Desmond Miles
Release: Limited to the Brotherhood

ANIMUS 3.0

Developer: Assassin Brotherhood
Launch date: 2012
Presence of subject analyzed: Mandatory
Risk of Bleeding Effect: High
Known user: Desmond Miles
Release: Limited to the Brotherhood

MONROE ANIMUS

Launch date: 2016
Developer: Sebastian Monroe, a former Abstergo employee, following technology theft.
Known users: Owen, Javier, Grace, Natalya, and David

ANIMUS CONSOLE

Developer: Abstergo Entertainment
Launch date: 2012
Presence of subject analyzed: Unnecessary thanks to Helix technology
Simulation reality: Full-scale monuments
Properties: Portable console for the general public. It was used to both create a positive view of the Templars in history and gather genetic information on its users.
Release: General public

ANIMUS OMEGA

Developer: Abstergo Entertainment
Launch date: 2012
Presence of subject analyzed: Unnecessary
Properties: Allows the user to relive their own memories and those of any other individual.
Release: Restricted to Abstergo employees

ANIMUS MOBILE

Developer: Abstergo Entertainment
Launch date: Unknown
Presence of subject analyzed: Unnecessary
Properties: Can be used on any smartphone. By connecting to the Helix servers of Abstergo, it can launch simulations of a selection of genetic memories.
Release: General public

BRAHMAN VR

Developer: Abstergo Entertainment and distributed by MysoreTech
Launch date: 2013
Presence of subject analyzed: Unnecessary
Properties: Games console with virtual reality headset. It also acts as a surveillance device for Abstergo, sending the genetic information of users to the cloud.
Known user: Jot Soora
Release: General public, Asian market

RISKS

WARNING! Desynchronization can lead to:

- mental confusion (Desmond)
- multiple personality disorder (Daniel Cross)
- complete mental breakdown (Charlotte de la Cruz)

ANIMI 4.3 AND 4.35

Developer: Abstergo Entertainment
Launch date: 2015-16
Presence of subject analyzed: Mandatory
Properties: The subject can be holographically projected into a simulation of an ancestor's past, whereas previous versions allowed the user to only view the simulation. The user is suspended from a giant mechanical arm connected to the machinery of the Animus to give the subject "full immersion" in the simulation.
Release: Restricted to Abstergo Madrid for 4.3 and London for 4.35
Known users: Simon Hathaway (Templar and member of the Inner Sanctum), and Callum Lynch

LIMITATIONS

For the simulation to work, it has to be stabilized through perfect synchronization between the user and historical subject—in other words, repeating the main actions, assassinations, and certain rites such as the Leaps of Faith. If desynchronization occurs, the simulation stops, with varying degrees of danger for the user. The user is sometimes exposed to moral conflicts when they are required to repeat certain actions of their ancestors of which they do not approve (as in the case of Charlotte de la Cruz and Thomas Stoddard).

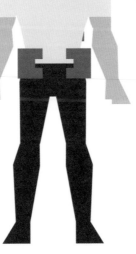

DDS

DATA DUMP SCANNER (DDS)

Software connected to the Animus used to relive already extracted memories without the user and owner of the memory having to be from the same bloodline. Invented by Abstergo Industries who used it in Project Legacy to obtain information on the Assassins and Pieces of Eden, and to train their agents via the Animi Training Program.

HELIX

HELIX

Technology developed by Abstergo Entertainment.

The genetic memories of any person can be explored. Users are no longer required to be prisoners of the Animus to read their own memories. Abstergo employees and even video game players are now used to look for artifacts.

The Helix is cloud-based gaming software developed by Abstergo with the official aim of allowing users to relive key historical periods. In reality, as well as acting as historical propaganda, it is used to amass huge quantities of data on users.

MEMORIES AVAILABLE IN HELIX 1.0

- The Tragedy of Jacques de Molay
- Triumph of the Borgias
- The Lone Eagle
- Murder in the Levant
- The Emperor's Shadow
- Fear and Loathing in Florence
- Washington and the Wolf
- The Liberation of Lady Aveline
- Devils of the Caribbean
- The Bladed Cross
- Jazz Age Junkies
- Hell in Hibernia

Like all computer programs, the Animus and Helix can be affected by bugs and hacking. Subject 16 hid secrets on the origins of humanity and Juno herself wanted to manipulate the simulation.

⊗ Assassin's Creed II

Problem type: Hacking

Description: 20 Glyphs hidden by Subject 16 can be used to discover that Adam and Eve are the first Assassins who rebelled against the Isu.

⊗ Assassin's Creed Brotherhood

Problem type: Hacking

Description: 10 hidden Glyphs unblock a level allowing Desmond to meet the consciousness of Subject 16.

⊗ Assassin's Creed Unity

Problem type: Bug

Description: Bugs in the Helix software send the user to different historical periods in Paris:

- Medieval Bastille
- Belle Époque
- Eiffel Tower under the German Occupation

⊗ Assassin's Creed IV Black Flag

Problem type: Hacking

Description: From October to December 2013, John Standish, head of the IT department at Abstergo Entertainment's Montreal facility, controlled an Abstergo research analyst to hack the Animus and reveal a large number of confidential documents.

⊗ Assassin's Creed Syndicate

Problem type: Hacking

Description: Juno hacks the simulation and makes the player relive a memory of Lydia Frye, granddaughter of Jacob Frye, in First World War London. Juno does this to try to recruit volunteers into the cult of her worshipers who want to bring her back to life.

⊗ Assassin's Creed Uprising

Problem type: Hacking

Description: Juno scans the mind of Charlotte de la Cruz in the simulation.

SUBJECTS

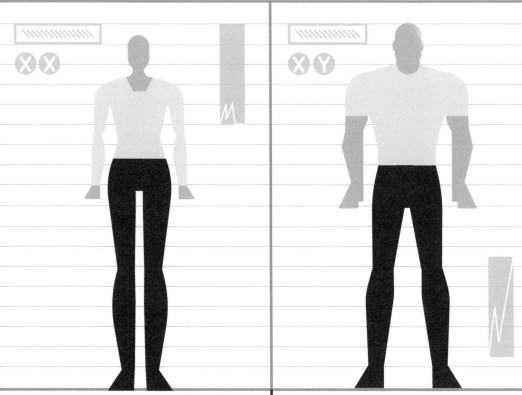

SUBJECT 0
Identity: Aileen Bock
(?-2013?)

SUBJECT 1
Identity: Unknown
(?-Jan 1981)

Aileen Bock ran the Abstergo Industries Surrogate Initiative. The aim of this project was to explore the genetic memories of historical individuals not directly related to the subject through DNA samples. By using the DNA of her son Seamus, she relived the memories of her ex-husband's mother, Miriam Kurtz, a prisoner of the Nazis in the Second World War.

The very first participant in the experimental phase of the Animus Project.
He was able to relive the memories of Aveline de Grandpré.

Before the creation of Helix technology, only the genetic memories of the person installed in the Animus could be explored. For many decades Abstergo therefore abducted and used people—whether Templars, Assassins, or unknown persons—whose ancestors could further its research. These are the Subjects—most of whose identities are unknown.

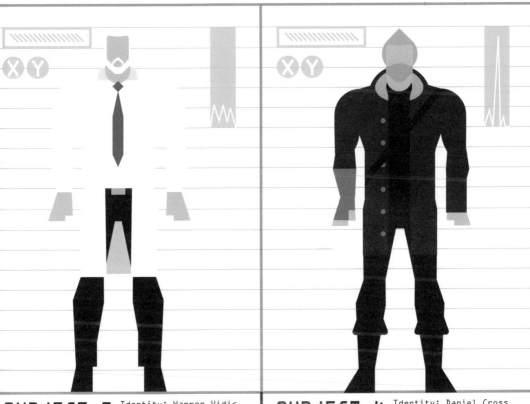

SUBJECT 2
Identity: Warren Vidic
(?-14 Dec 2012)

Positions held included head of the Abstergo research department. Here he was able to relive the memories of his ancestor, Geoffroy Thérage, executioner of Joan of Arc.

SUBJECT 4
Identity: Daniel Cross
(09 Mar 1974-14 Dec 2012)

The great-grandson of Assassin Nikolaï Orelov, Daniel Cross becomes an infiltrator for Abstergo after his abduction by them. He successfully infiltrates the headquarters of the Assassins in Dubai and kills their mentor. He captures Desmond Miles and delivers him to Abstergo.

Desmond eliminates him during their confrontation in Rome on 14th December 2012.

SUBJECTS

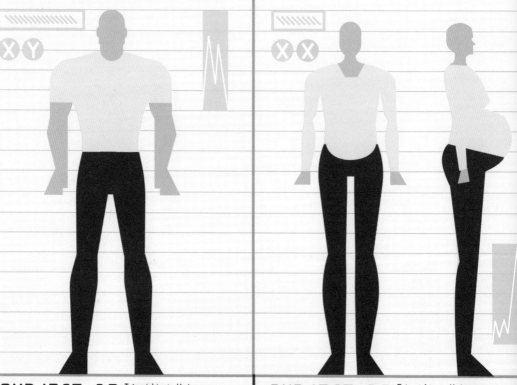

SUBJECT 12
Identity: Unknown
(?-?)

A male who experienced serious problems as a result of the Bleeding Effect caused by the Animus.

SUBJECT 15
Identity: Unknown
(?-14 Dec 2010)

By reading the genetic memory of the subject's fetus, the Animus was able to access the memories of the child's mother and father at the same time.

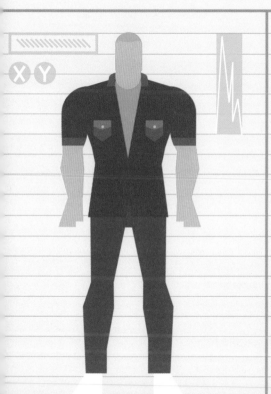

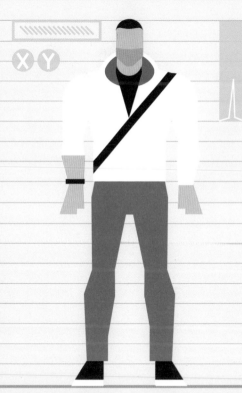

SUBJECT 16
Identity: Clay Kaczmarek
(1982-08 Aug 2012)

An Assassin given the mission of infiltrating Abstergo and finding out more about the Animus. He was adversely affected by the many Animus sessions and was eventually unable to separate his own consciousness from his ancestors. He is alleged to have committed suicide but his consciousness remains in the Animus. He was responsible for organizing the information leaks in the Animus and helped Desmond emerge from his coma.

SUBJECT 17
Identity: Desmond Miles
(13 Mar 1987-21 Dec 2012)

A male captured by Abstergo for his famous Assassin ancestors, most notably, Aquilus, Altaïr Ibn-La'Ahad, Ezio Auditore, Edward Kenway, and Ratonhnhaké:ton (Connor). He joins the ranks of the Assassins and eventually sacrifices himself to save humanity.

DESMOND MILES
SUBJECT 17 (1987-2012)

A direct descendant of famous Assassins from all over the world, Desmond was abducted by Abstergo to acquire an Apple of Eden that his ancestors must have had in their possession.

 Born 13th March 1987 at "the Farm," an Assassin secret compound in South Dakota (United States).

♀ Mother: Unknown.

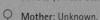 ♂ Father: William Miles, a central figure in the modern Assassin Brotherhood.

Son: Elijah, born in 2005, although Desmond has never known of his existence. Although Elijah is a Sage, he appears to have inherited the obstinacy and willpower of his father.

INFORMATION:

- Descendant of Altaïr, Ezio, and the Kenway bloodline (Edward–Haytham–Connor)

- Sacrifices himself to save humanity

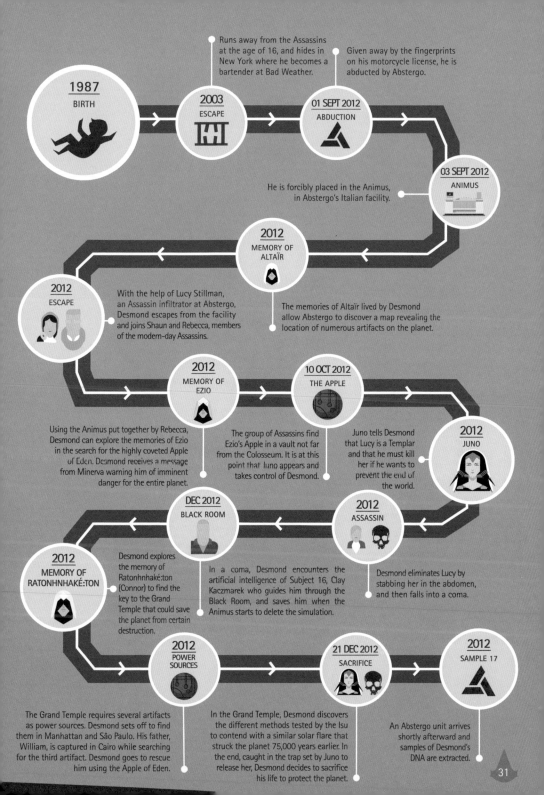

1987 BIRTH

2003 ESCAPE

Runs away from the Assassins at the age of 16, and hides in New York where he becomes a bartender at Bad Weather.

01 SEPT 2012 ABDUCTION

Given away by the fingerprints on his motorcycle license, he is abducted by Abstergo.

03 SEPT 2012 ANIMUS

He is forcibly placed in the Animus, in Abstergo's Italian facility.

2012 MEMORY OF ALTAÏR

The memories of Altaïr lived by Desmond allow Abstergo to discover a map revealing the location of numerous artifacts on the planet.

2012 ESCAPE

With the help of Lucy Stillman, an Assassin infiltrator at Abstergo, Desmond escapes from the facility and joins Shaun and Rebecca, members of the modern-day Assassins.

2012 MEMORY OF EZIO

Using the Animus put together by Rebecca, Desmond can explore the memories of Ezio in the search for the highly coveted Apple of Eden. Desmond receives a message from Minerva warning him of imminent danger for the entire planet.

10 OCT 2012 THE APPLE

The group of Assassins find Ezio's Apple in a vault not far from the Colosseum. It is at this point that Juno appears and takes control of Desmond.

2012 JUNO

Juno tells Desmond that Lucy is a Templar and that he must kill her if he wants to prevent the end of the world.

DEC 2012 BLACK ROOM

Desmond explores the memory of Ratonhnhaké:ton (Connor) to find the key to the Grand Temple that could save the planet from certain destruction.

In a coma, Desmond encounters the artificial intelligence of Subject 16, Clay Kaczmarek who guides him through the Black Room, and saves him when the Animus starts to delete the simulation.

2012 ASSASSIN

Desmond eliminates Lucy by stabbing her in the abdomen, and then falls into a coma.

2012 MEMORY OF RATONHNHAKÉ:TON

2012 POWER SOURCES

The Grand Temple requires several artifacts as power sources. Desmond sets off to find them in Manhattan and São Paulo. His father, William, is captured in Cairo while searching for the third artifact. Desmond goes to rescue him using the Apple of Eden.

21 DEC 2012 SACRIFICE

In the Grand Temple, Desmond discovers the different methods tested by the Isu to contend with a similar solar flare that struck the planet 75,000 years earlier. In the end, caught in the trap set by Juno to release her, Desmond decides to sacrifice his life to protect the planet.

2012 SAMPLE 17

An Abstergo unit arrives shortly afterward and samples of Desmond's DNA are extracted.

DESMOND'S GENEALOGY

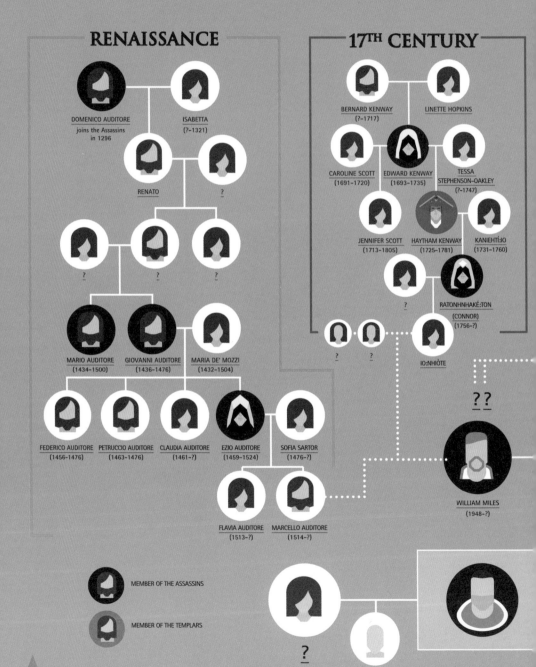

RENAISSANCE

DOMENICO AUDITORE
joins the Assassins in 1296

ISABETTA
(?–1321)

RENATO

?

?

?

?

MARIO AUDITORE
(1434–1500)

GIOVANNI AUDITORE
(1436–1476)

MARIA DE' MOZZI
(1432–1504)

FEDERICO AUDITORE
(1456–1476)

PETRUCCIO AUDITORE
(1463–1476)

CLAUDIA AUDITORE
(1461–?)

EZIO AUDITORE
(1459–1524)

SOFIA SARTOR
(1476–?)

FLAVIA AUDITORE
(1513–?)

MARCELLO AUDITORE
(1514–?)

17TH CENTURY

BERNARD KENWAY
(?–1717)

LINETTE HOPKINS

CAROLINE SCOTT
(1691–1720)

EDWARD KENWAY
(1693–1735)

TESSA STEPHENSON-OAKLEY
(?–1747)

JENNIFER SCOTT
(1713–1805)

HAYTHAM KENWAY
(1725–1781)

KANIEHTÍ:IO
(1731–1760)

?

RATONHNHAKÉ:TON
(CONNOR)
(1756–?)

?

?

IO:NHIÓTE

??

WILLIAM MILES
(1948–?)

?

ELIJAH
(2005–)

MEMBER OF THE ASSASSINS

MEMBER OF THE TEMPLARS

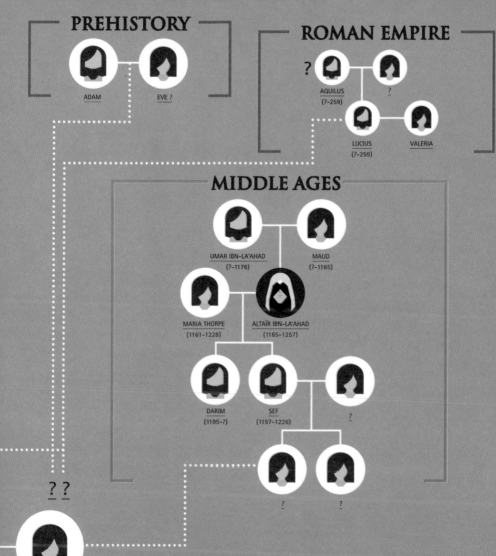

PREHISTORY

ADAM

EVE ?

ROMAN EMPIRE

?

AQUILUS
(?-259)

?

LUCIUS
(?-259)

VALERIA

MIDDLE AGES

UMAR IBN–LA'AHAD
(?-1176)

MAUD
(?-1165)

MARIA THORPE
(1161-1228)

ALTAÏR IBN–LA'AHAD
(1165-1257)

DARIM
(1195-?)

SEF
(1197-1226)

?

?

?

? ?

?

DESMOND MILES
(13 Mar 1987–21 Dec 2012)
Sacrificed himself in the Grand
Temple in Turin, New York State,
to prevent a global apocalypse.

Desmond is tracked down and then abducted by Abstergo for his exceptional genetic inheritance—his bloodline features numerous Assassins and other notable figures. By rereading the memories of his ancestors, both the Assassins and Templars hope to find the artifacts of the First Civilization.

33

TEMPLAR HALL OF FAME

ROBERT DE SABLÉ
(1150–1191) Holy Land
Robert de Sablé, lord of Anjou (a region of France under English rule), is the 11th Grand Master of the Templars of the Levantine Rite, from 1190 until his death in 1191.

JACQUES DE MOLAY
(1224–1314) France
The last official Grand Master of the Knights Templar, burned at the stake by King Philip IV of France. Following his death, the Templar Order goes underground.

Templar Grand Master

Member of the Templars

RODRIGO BORGIA
(1431–1503) Italy
Elected Pope Alexander VI in 1492 and Grand Master of the Templars from 1476 until his death in 1503. He retrieves an artifact in the Vatican and discovers an Apple of Eden in Cyprus, which Ezio eventually steals from him.

LAUREANO DE TORRES Y AYALA
(1645–1722) Caribbean
Grand Master of the Templar Order in the Caribbean, living in Havana. He is responsible for locating the Observatory, which can be used to spy on anyone on the planet.

HAYTHAM KENWAY
(1725–1781) England & US
The son of pirate Assassin Edward Kenway, and father of Ratonhnhaké:ton (Connor), Haytham establishes the Templar rite in North America and discovers the location of the Grand Temple.

TEMPLAR HALL
OF FAME

SHAY CORMAC
(1731-?) US & Canada

Shocked by Achilles Davenport's lack of concern over the deaths of innocents, Assassin Shay decides to join the Templars. He kills Arno Dorian's father in Versailles and recovers the Precursor box.

ÉLISE DE LA SERRE
(1768-1794) France

Daughter of Grand Master François de la Serre who was killed following a coup in the French Order during the Revolution. She tries to find the person responsible for her father's assassination with the help of Arno Dorian. She dies while eliminating him.

FRANÇOIS-THOMAS GERMAIN
(1726-1794) France

Silversmith to the King of France and Grand Master of the Order during the French Revolution, he leads a coup against François de la Serre and manipulates political events to increase Templar influence in the country.

Templar Grand Master

Member of the Templars

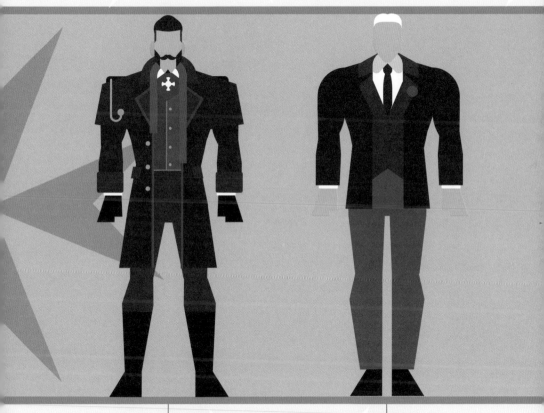

CRAWFORD STARRICK
(1827-1868) UK
A ruthless businessman and Grand
Master of the British Order during the
Victorian period, he controls London
with an iron fist. He is killed by the Frye
twins despite his having acquired the
Shroud of Eden.

HENRY FORD
(1863-1947) US
American businessman responsible
for the brutal expansion of capitalism,
thanks to improvements in mass-
production techniques in his factories.
He is one of the founders of Abstergo
Industries in 1937.

CLASH OF
IDEOLOGIES

 ## ASSASSINS

V

FREEDOM

- BELIEF IN THE FREE WILL OF HUMANITY SINCE ITS LIBERATION FROM THE ISU BY ADAM AND EVE.

- HUMANITY MUST FREE ITSELF OF ALL CONSTRAINTS.

- LIBERTARIAN TENDENCIES.

- FRAGMENTED ORGANIZATION WITHOUT AN INTEGRATED COMMON COMMAND. RISK OF BLIND FAITH IN THE CREED.

NOT SO SIMPLE . . .

 Shay Cormac, a former Assassin turned Templar, questions blind faith in the Creed and its consequences in terms of its cost to human life.

 Followers of alternative ideologies include: for example, the Instruments of the First Will. The aim of this group is to return Juno to her physical form and establish a New World Order dominated by the Isu. In this world, humans would revert to being the slaves of the Isu.

RECONC

FRENCH REVOLUTION

For the good of the country and with the aim of establishing a more democratic political organization, Templar Grand Master de la Serre and Assassin Mentor Mirabeau decide to implement a truce. This period is also a time of reconciliation between Templar Élise de la Serre and Assassin Arno Dorian. The love they have for each other makes them reassess the limitations of their respective Orders.

Assassins kill for freedom, and Templars want to control humanity to make it greater. There are numerous contradictions, and no one has an undisputed claim over good or evil. While the two factions are ideologically opposed to each other, the actions of some of their members occasionally blur the lines.

S TEMPLARS

EFFICIENCY

- BELIEF IN CONTROL, EVEN IF IT MEANS CONSTRAINING HUMANITY THROUGH USE OF THE PIECES OF EDEN.

- HUMANITY MUST BE GUIDED TO REACH A CERTAIN LEVEL OF PERFECTION.

- AUTHORITARIAN TENDENCIES AND VIEW FREE WILL AS DEVIANCE LEADING TO CHAOS.

- VERTICAL ORGANIZATION, CULT OF SECRECY, PULLING OF STRINGS BEHIND THE SCENES. ACCEPT SACRIFICES FOR THE GREATER GOOD OF HUMANITY.

NOT SO SIMPLE . . .

Laureano de Torres y Ayala (1645-1722), Templar Grand Master, declares himself against slavery and the mistreatment of slaves.

To prevent any corruption and stop Templar Grand Masters from flouting the precepts of the Order, the Inner Sanctum created the position of the Black Cross. None of the characters know the identity of the Black Cross, not even the nine members of the Inner Sanctum. Since 2016 the position has been held by Juhani Otso Berg.

ILIATION

BATTLE AGAINST JUNO

The threat of the return of Juno in our era is redrawing the battle lines, and the two sides will have to unite to ensure that humanity does not fall under the rule of the Isu.

ASSASSIN HALL OF FAME

EZIO AUDITORE
(1459–1524)

Period: Renaissance
Opponents: Rodrigo Borgia
and Cesare Borgia
Pieces of Eden: Apple of Eden
and Memory Seals
Motivation: Vengeance
Attributes: Known as the Prophet

EDWARD KENWAY
(1693–1735)

Period: War of the Spanish Succession
Opponent: Laureano de Torres y Ayala
Pieces of Eden: Crystal Skull
Motivation: Adventure
Attributes: Pirate

RATONHNHAKÉ:TON (CONNOR)
(1756–?)

Period: American Revolution
Opponent: Charles Lee
Pieces of Eden: Apple of Eden
and Kidd's Shard of Eden
Motivation: Justice
Attributes: Native American

(1847-?)

Period: Industrial Revolution
Opponent: Crawford Starrick
Pieces of Eden: Shroud of Eden
Motivation: Ego
Attributes: Knighted by
Queen Victoria

EVIE FRYE
(1847-?)

Period: Industrial Revolution
Opponent: Crawford Starrick
Pieces of Eden: Shroud of Eden
Motivation: Duty
Attributes: Knighted by
Queen Victoria

NIKOLAÏ ORELOV
(?-1928)

Period: Russian Revolution
Opponent: Tsar Alexander III
Pieces of Eden: Staff of Eden
Motivation: Duty

ASSASSIN HALL OF FAME

ARNO DORIAN
(1768-?)

Period: French Revolution
Opponent: François-Thomas Germain
Pieces of Eden: Sword of Eden
and Apple of Eden
Motivation: Redemption
Attributes: Escapes from the
Bastille on 14th July 1789

AVELINE DE GRANDPRÉ
(1747-?)

Period: Seven Years' War
Opponent: Madeleine de l'Isle
Pieces of Eden: Prophecy Disk
Motivation: Justice
Attributes: Mistress
of disguise

ALTAÏR IBN-LA'AHAD
(1165-1257)

Period: Third Crusade
Opponent: Al Mualim
Pieces of Eden: Apple of Eden
Motivation: Duty
Attributes: Reformer of
the Creed

BAYEK
(1st century BCE)

Period: Roman Egypt
Opponent: The Snake
Pieces of Eden: Apple of Eden
and Staff of Eden
Motivation: Vengeance, then idealism
Attributes: Medjay, protector
of Cleopatra

SHAO JUN
(1505-?)

Period: 16th-century China
Opponent: The Jiajing Emperor
Pieces of Eden: Precursor box
Motivation: Vengeance and idealism

ARBAAZ MIR
(19th century)

Period: British India
Opponent: Francis Cotton
Pieces of Eden: Koh-i-Noor
Motivation: Protection
Attributes: Only Assassin to
own a Trident Blade

HIDDEN BLADES

"The Hidden Blade has been a constant companion of ours over the years. Some would say it defines us—and they would not be entirely wrong. Many of our successes would not have been possible without it." Altaïr Ibn-La'Ahad's Codex.

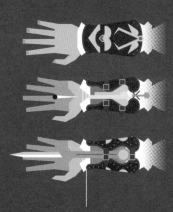

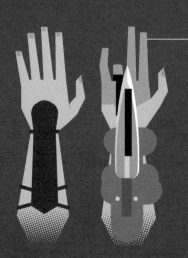

ORIGINAL BLADE

First recorded use in the 5th century BCE, in the assassination of King Xerxes I by Darius, a member of the Persian Brotherhood.

Users: Darius and Bayek

EZIO'S BLADE

In addition to the attributes of the original blade, thanks to improvements made by Leonardo da Vinci it can:

- infect with poison
- fire darts and bullets

User: Ezio

HOOKBLADE

An improvement used by the Ottoman Brotherhood of Constantinople in the 16th century. It can be used on the network of ziplines in the city to move around or escape more quickly. The hook also enables the wearer to climb swiftly when scaling buildings.

User: Ezio

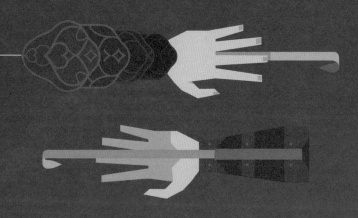

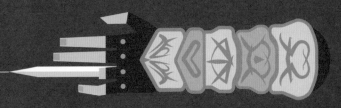

ALTAÏR'S BLADE

Altaïr makes some modifications
so that amputation of the user's
ring finger is no longer required.

User: Altaïr

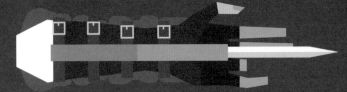

PIVOT BLADE

The blade pivots so that it can be wielded like a dagger.

Users: Achilles Davenport then Ratonhnhaké:ton (Connor)

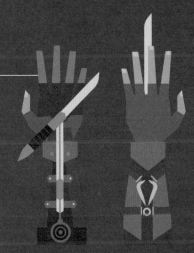

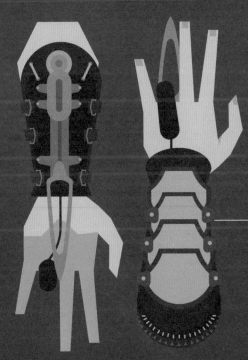

BAYEK'S BLADE

The model used by Bayek is very
similar to the original blade.

User: Bayek

HIDDEN BLADES

TRIDENT BLADE

This is the first and only known example of a Trident Blade.

User: Arbaaz Mir

ASSASSIN GAUNTLET

As well as the Hidden Blade, this multifunctional glove also contains poison darts and a grappling hook for extremely fast climbing of buildings.

Users: Jacob and Evie Frye

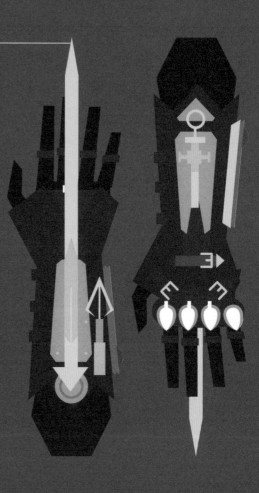

PHANTOM BLADE

This blade contains a mechanism similar to a crossbow.

User: Arno Dorian

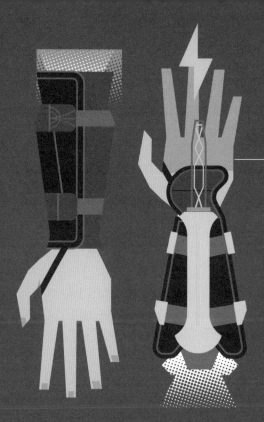

SHOCK BLADE

This Hidden Blade combines a classic blade
and a system that discharges electricity.

Users: Rebecca Crane
and Shaun Hastings

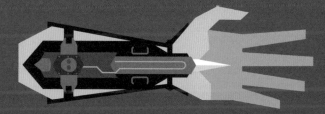

DUNCAN WALPOLE'S BLADE

Blade recovered from the corpse
of Assassin Duncan Walpole.

Users: Duncan Walpole
then Edward Kenway

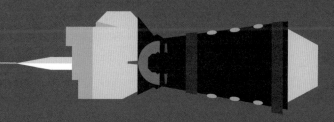

THE LEAP OF FAITH

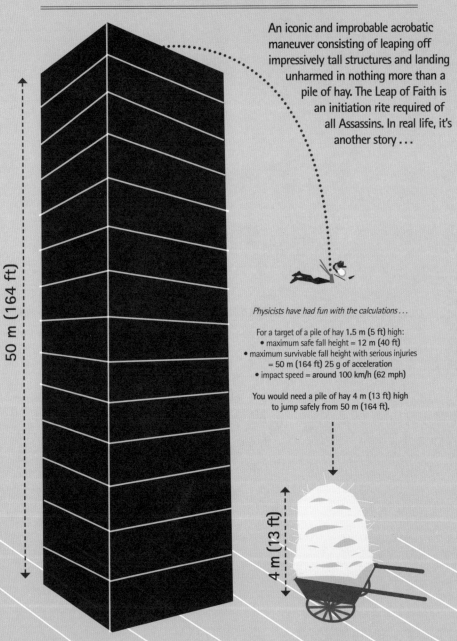

An iconic and improbable acrobatic maneuver consisting of leaping off impressively tall structures and landing unharmed in nothing more than a pile of hay. The Leap of Faith is an initiation rite required of all Assassins. In real life, it's another story . . .

50 m (164 ft)

Physicists have had fun with the calculations . . .

For a target of a pile of hay **1.5 m (5 ft)** high:
- maximum safe fall height = 12 m (40 ft)
- maximum survivable fall height with serious injuries = 50 m (164 ft) 25 g of acceleration
- impact speed = around 100 km/h (62 mph)

You would need a pile of hay 4 m (13 ft) high to jump safely from 50 m (164 ft).

4 m (13 ft)

NUMBER OF JUMPS PER ASSASSIN*

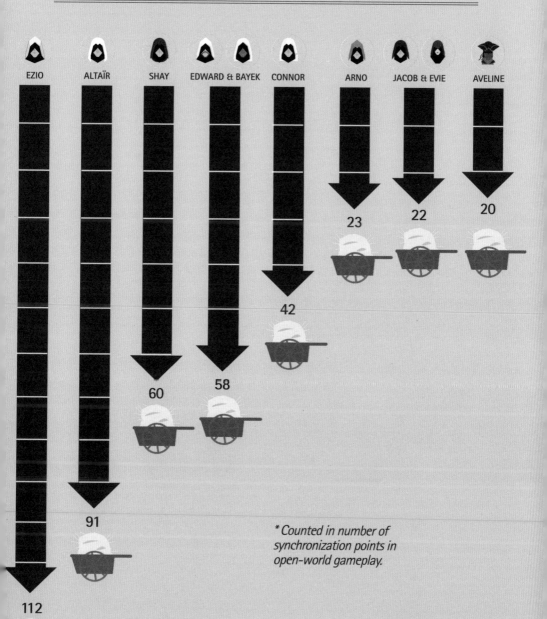

EZIO — 112

ALTAÏR — 91

SHAY — 60

EDWARD & BAYEK — 58

CONNOR — 42

ARNO — 23

JACOB & EVIE — 22

AVELINE — 20

Counted in number of synchronization points in open-world gameplay.

A BIT OF CLIMBING!

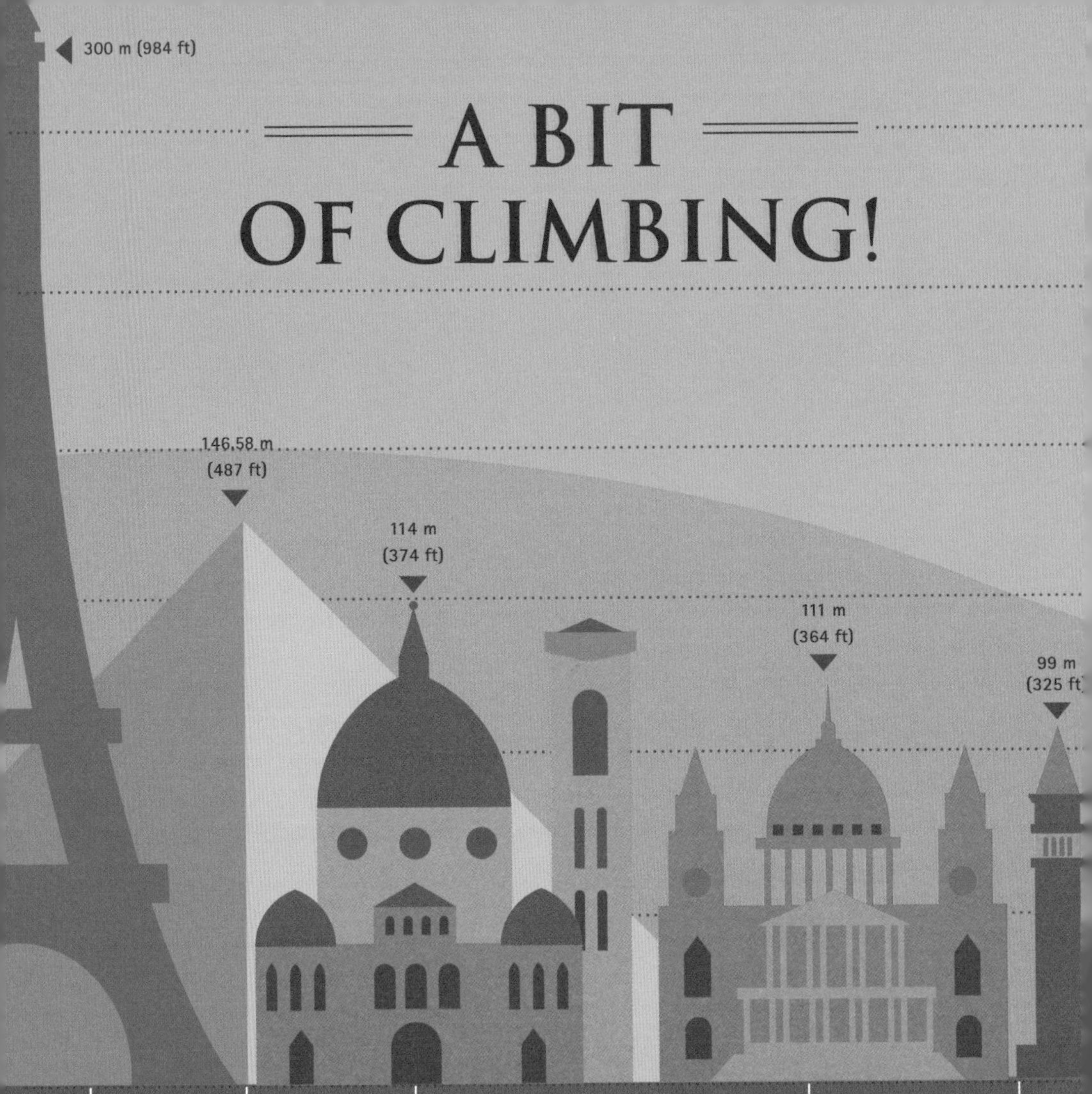

146.58 m
(487 ft)

114 m
(374 ft)

111 m
(364 ft)

99 m
(325 ft)

EIFFEL TOWER
Paris
(AC Unity)

⚐ *Arno Dorian*
🕐 *Second World War*
❓ *Arno accesses it via a time warp*

PYRAMID OF CHEOPS
Giza
(AC Origins)

⚐ *Bayek*
🕐 *49 BCE*

SANTA MARIA DEL FIORE
Florence
(AC II)

⚐ *Ezio*
🕐 *1476*
❓ *Contains the tomb of the ancient Assassin Iltani*

ST PAUL'S CATHEDRAL
London
(AC Syndicate)

⚐ *Frye twins*
🕐 *1868*
❓ *Used to hide a necklace from the First Civilization*

CAMPANILE DI SAN MARCO
Venice
(AC II)

⚐ *Ezio*
🕐 *1481*
❓ *The highest building in the city; it contains a Glyph*

Monuments are other essential elements of the historical tourism allowed by the games, and are reproduced as faithfully as possible in each of the episodes. Scaled down by 20% until AC Unity, they have since been depicted to scale.

○ Monuments depicted to scale in the game; the others are reduced by 20%.

⚲ Climbed by

🕐 Period

? Attributes

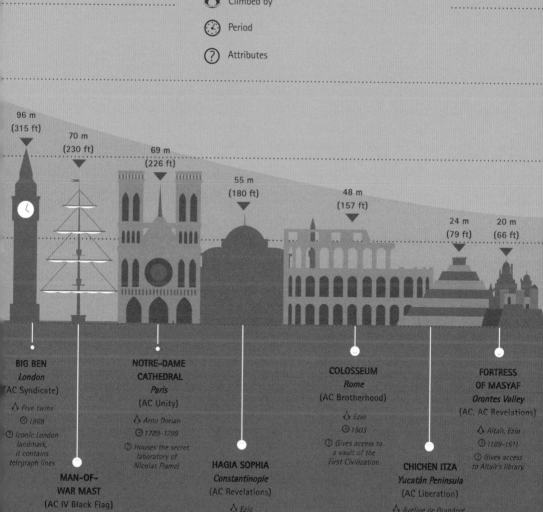

96 m (315 ft)

70 m (230 ft)

69 m (226 ft)

55 m (180 ft)

48 m (157 ft)

24 m (79 ft)

20 m (66 ft)

BIG BEN
London
(AC Syndicate)

⚲ *Frye twins*
🕐 *1868*
? *Iconic London landmark, it contains telegraph lines*

MAN-OF-WAR MAST
(AC IV Black Flag)

⚲ *Edward Kenway*
🕐 *1713-1723*
? *Heavily armed warship*

NOTRE-DAME CATHEDRAL
Paris
(AC Unity)

⚲ *Arno Dorian*
🕐 *1789-1799*
? *Houses the secret laboratory of Nicolas Flamel*

HAGIA SOPHIA
Constantinople
(AC Revelations)

⚲ *Ezio*
🕐 *1511*
? *Contains the tomb of Ishak Pasha*

COLOSSEUM
Rome
(AC Brotherhood)

⚲ *Ezio*
🕐 *1503*
? *Gives access to a vault of the First Civilization*

CHICHEN ITZA
Yucatán Peninsula
(AC Liberation)

⚲ *Aveline de Grandpré*
🕐 *1769*
? *A temple of the First Civilization*

FORTRESS OF MASYAF
Orontes Valley
(AC, AC Revelations)

⚲ *Altaïr, Ezio*
🕐 *1189-1511*
? *Gives access to Altaïr's library.*

CRESTS

ASSASSIN'S CREED

Some see a resemblance with the Freemason symbols of the square and compass, while for others it represents the talons of an eagle, or quite simply . . . the A of Assassin!

ASSASSIN'S CREED BROTHERHOOD

An intricate crest symbolizing the Renaissance in all its flamboyance.

ASSASSIN'S CREED IV
BLACK FLAG

This crest is the emblem of Edward Kenway, the Assassin pirate, and flutters at the top of the *Jackdaw*. It perfectly combines two symbols for an eye-catching result!

ASSASSIN'S CREED CHRONICLES: RUSSIA

This crest skillfully takes up the graphic imagery of Soviet Russia.

ASSASSIN'S CREED SYNDICATE

The Assassins carry out their own industrial revolution with this mechanically themed crest featuring rivets.

The insignia of the Assassin Order has changed many times to reflect different historical periods and games.

ASSASSIN'S CREED REVELATIONS

The crest of the Ottoman Brotherhood, designed by brothers Niccolò and Maffeo Polo in Constantinople in 1258, borrows both from Byzantine art and the Ottoman influences on Constantinople.

ASSASSIN'S CREED ROGUE

The crest here is split and broken, reflecting the destiny of the game's hero, Shay Cormac, an Assassin turned Templar. It also evokes images of the Lisbon Earthquake and the ice fields of the Arctic.

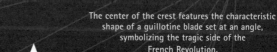

ASSASSIN'S CREED UNITY

The center of the crest features the characteristic shape of a guillotine blade set at an angle, symbolizing the tragic side of the French Revolution.

ASSASSIN'S CREED ORIGINS

Here the crest is cleverly completed with the Eye of Horus from ancient Egypt, that symbolizes light and knowledge. The Eye of Horus is also the symbol worn by Bayek as a Medjay.

HAVE WE MET?

JULIUS CAESAR
(100 BCE – 44 BCE)

The Roman senator is looking for the artifacts used by Alexander the Great to establish his own power. He dies in Rome from the blows wielded by Aya, Brutus, and the rebel senators.

Appearance: AC Origins

AL MUALIM
(1135 – 1191)

ROBERT DE SABLÉ
(1150 – 1193)

Rashid ad-Din Sinan, known as Al Mualim, is leader of the Levantine Assassins from 1163. Betraying the Brotherhood, he is eliminated by Altaïr in 1191.

Appearances:
AC, AC Revelations

Robert de Sablé, lord of Anjou—a region of France under English rule—is the 11th Grand Master of the Templars of the Levantine Rite, from 1190 until his death in 1191.

Appearance:
AC

| 200 BCE | 100 BCE | 50 BCE | YEAR 0 | 500 | 1000 | 1100 |

CLEOPATRA, QUEEN OF EGYPT
(69 BCE – 30 BCE)

Assassins Bayek and Aya provide direct assistance to the Queen of Egypt in her struggle to take back her throne from her brother, Ptolemy XIII. She then betrays them, preferring the protection of Caesar and the Order of the Ancients.

Appearance:
AC Origins

PTOLEMY XIII, PHARAOH OF EGYPT
(62 BCE – 47 BCE)

As a young teenager of 13, he removes his sister Cleopatra from power in order to reign alone. He is devoured by a crocodile while trying to escape in the Battle of the Nile.

Appearance:
AC Origins

RICHARD THE LIONHEART
(1157 – 1199)

Richard I of England, leader of the Third Crusade to the Holy Land. He eventually makes peace with Saladin when he discovers the treason of Templar Robert de Sablé, eliminated by Altaïr.

Appearance:
AC

LEONARDO DA VINCI
(1452–1519)

Brilliant inventor and artist. His patrons include the Auditore family, and he makes friends with Ezio. He deciphers Altaïr's Codex for Ezio and makes him weapons and gadgets.

Appearances: AC II, AC Brotherhood

Each episode of the game allows the player to encounter key figures from history and to see them in a new light. Whether friends or enemies, these great names have crossed paths with the Assassins. Discover the most important ones here.

- ♠ Assassin sympathizer
- ♠ Member of the Assassins
- ● Neutral figure
- ✳ Templar sympathizer
- ✳ Member of the Templars

SULEIMAN
(1494–1566)

The future great Sultan is still only a prince when he crosses paths with Ezio in Constantinople.

Appearance:
AC Revelations

BLACKBEARD
(1680–1718)

With the real name of Edward Thatch, he is the most famous pirate of the Caribbean. His close friend Assassin Edward Kenway is unable to save him from an attack by the British in 1718.

Appearance: AC IV Black Flag

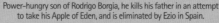
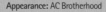

RODRIGO BORGIA
(1431–1503)

Pope Alexander VI and Grand Master of the Templars during the Renaissance. He retrieves an artifact from the Vatican and discovers an Apple of Eden in Cyprus, which Ezio eventually steals from him.

Appearances:
AC II, AC Brotherhood

LUCREZIA BORGIA
(1480–1519)

Daughter of Rodrigo Borgia, she assists him and her brother, Cesare, in the conquest of Rome. She imprisons Caterina Sforza in the Castel Sant'Angelo.

Appearance:
AC Brotherhood

CESARE BORGIA
(1475–1507)

Power-hungry son of Rodrigo Borgia, he kills his father in an attempt to take his Apple of Eden, and is eliminated by Ezio in Spain.

Appearance: AC Brotherhood

GEORGE WASHINGTON
(1732–1799)

General of the rebel American colonies, and one of the Founding Fathers of the United States. He is responsible for the destruction of the native village of Ratonhnhaké:ton (Connor). He refuses to use the Apple of Eden for his own profit.

Appearances: AC III, AC Rogue

MAXIMILIEN DE ROBESPIERRE
(1758–1794)

An idealistic revolutionary, he is brought to power by Templar Grand Master François-Thomas Germain in exchange for implementing the Reign of Terror in Paris.

Appearance: AC Unity

NAPOLEON BONAPARTE
(1769–1821)

The young Napoleon tracks down an Apple of Eden, but the Assassin Arno Dorian retrieves it and sends it to Egypt. Napoleon then goes to Egypt to collect the Apple for himself.

Appearance: AC Unity

1750

1800

1850

BENJAMIN FRANKLIN
(1706–1790)

Scientist, author, and politician, Benjamin Franklin is one of the Founding Fathers of the United States. Templar Haytham Kenway finds the stolen pages of his Almanac.

Appearances: AC III, AC Rogue

COMTE DE MIRABEAU
(1749–1791)

Politician and deputy of the Third Estate during the French Revolution. As Mentor of the French Brotherhood of Assassins, he attempts to introduce a truce with the Templars to change the political system of the country.

Appearance: AC Unity

MARQUIS DE SADE
(1740–1814)

Libertine aristocrat imprisoned in the Bastille, he uses Arno Dorian to become the leader of the slum known as the Cour des Miracles. He asks the Assassin to help him find the Head of Saint-Denis lantern.

Appearance: AC Unity

HAVE WE MET?

CHARLES DARWIN
(1809 – 1882)

English naturalist and geologist responsible for the theory of evolution, he uses the help of Jacob Frye to recover fossils and demolish a factory producing opium-based syrup.

Appearance:
AC Syndicate

QUEEN VICTORIA
(1819 – 1901)

To thank them for helping to save her life, Queen Victoria makes Jacob Frye a knight and Evie Frye a dame. She also entrusts them with occasional missions.

Appearance: AC Syndicate

1900

1950

ALEXANDER III,
EMPEROR OF RUSSIA
(1845 – 1894)

Tsar of Russia from 1881 until his death in 1894. His imposing stature and the Staff of Eden ensure total domination over his people.

Appearance:
AC The Fall (comic book)

💧	Assassin sympathizer
🔵	Member of the Assassins
✳	Templar sympathizer
✴	Member of the Templars
⚪	Neutral figure

CHAPTER 3
ASSASSIN HISTORIES

ALTAÏR IBN-LA'AHAD
THE REFORMER (1165-1257)

Mentor of the Brotherhood based in Masyaf, his study of an Apple of Eden is used to improve the weapons and techniques of the Assassins. He is also responsible for the expansion of the Brotherhood around the world and dissemination of its ideology through his Codex.

 Born into a family of Assassins

 Mother: Maud, died in

 childbirth

Father: Umar Ibn-La'Ahad, executed by the Saracens

THE NINE TARGETS OF ALTAÏR

- Tamir, arms dealer in Damascus
- Garnier de Naplouse, Grand Master of the Hospitaliers in Acre
- Talal, slaver in Jerusalem
- Abu'l Nuqoud, merchant king of Damascus
- William of Montferrat, regent of Acre
- Majd Addin, regent of Jerusalem
- Sibrand, leader of the Knights Teutonic, Acre
- Jubair al Hakim, Chief Scholar of Damascus
- Robert de Sablé, 11th Grand Master of the Templar Order

The Templars attack Masyaf. Altaïr saves the fortress single-handedly. Al Mualim appoints him Master Assassin.

Altaïr searches for an artifact known as the Chalice. In fact, it is a woman named Adha, with whom he falls in love. She is killed by the Templars, leaving Altaïr devastated.

11 JAN 1165
BIRTH

1189
MASTER ASSASSIN

1190
QUEST FOR THE CHALICE

1191
THIRD CRUSADE

Altaïr and a group of Assassins are sent by Al Mualim to the vault beneath Solomon's Temple in Jerusalem to retrieve an Apple of Eden.

QUEST FOR REDEMPTION

WOUNDED EGO

CONFRONTATION

Robert de Sablé reveals the existence of a tenth target: Al Mualim, who used Altaïr to eliminate any competition and keep the Apple for himself.

Mentor Al Mualim strips Altaïr of his rank and weapons. Altaïr has to eliminate nine targets to redeem himself.

Altaïr fails to retrieve the Apple of Eden from the hands of Robert de Sablé. Altaïr's arrogance also causes him to break the three tenets of the Creed.

SEPT 1191

1193

CODEX

At age 25, Altaïr eliminates Al Mualim and becomes the youngest ever Mentor of the Brotherhood. The Apple taken from Al Mualim projects a map of the Pieces of Eden spread over the planet.

Altaïr sets out to find the Templar Archive in Cyprus where he eliminates the new Grand Master Armand Bouchart.

Altaïr writes the Codex that sets out the new rules of the Brotherhood.

1228
COUP IN MASYAF

1217–1227
GENGHIS KHAN

REFUGE IN ALAMUT

Altaïr takes refuge in the fortress of Alamut, built over a First Civilization temple. He records his memories onto artifacts there.

Returning to Masyaf, Altaïr learns of the death of his friend Malik and Altaïr's son Sef is killed during a coup orchestrated by Abbas Sofian. Altaïr's wife dies the same year during the confrontation between Altaïr and Abbas.

The expansion of the Mongols threatens the Assassins. Altaïr, his wife (Maria), and Darim, one of his two sons, set off to confront Genghis Khan in China.

1247
RETURN TO MASYAF

LIBRARY

12 AUG 1257
DEATH

The elderly Altaïr manages to retake control of Masyaf with the assistance of young Assassins faithful to his cause.

Altaïr hands over his Codex and builds a library underneath the Masyaf fortress. He asks for the Assassin teachings to be spread around the world. He records his sixth and final memory onto a seal that is read by Ezio.

At age 92 Altaïr locks himself into his library to die alone with his Apple of Eden.

EZIO AUDITORE
THE PROPHET (1459-1524)

Ezio Auditore is undoubtedly the most charismatic Assassin and he is the only character whose life we follow through three different games. A young, carefree nobleman and inveterate seducer of women, he is driven by a desire for vengeance when his family is killed. Finding no solace in eliminating the Borgias, he begins a quest to study the origins of the Brotherhood and retraces the steps of Altaïr. Thanks to his friend Leonardo da Vinci, he deciphers Altaïr's Codex. He plays the role of Prophet by speaking with Minerva and hiding the Apple of Eden in the Colosseum Vault, so that Desmond can find it five centuries later.

Born 24th June 1459
in Florence

♀ Mother: Maria Auditore

♂ Father: Giovanni Auditore,
Assassin and banker

INFORMATION:

• Finds two Apples of Eden
and Altaïr's Codex

• Transmits messages from
Minerva to Desmond

• Mentor of the Italian
Brotherhood from 1503
to 1513

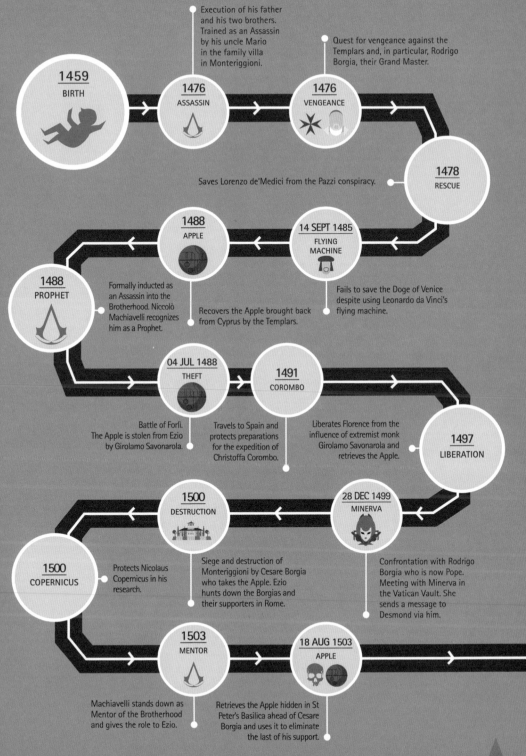

1459
BIRTH

1476
ASSASSIN

Execution of his father and his two brothers. Trained as an Assassin by his uncle Mario in the family villa in Monteriggioni.

1476
VENGEANCE

Quest for vengeance against the Templars and, in particular, Rodrigo Borgia, their Grand Master.

1478
RESCUE

Saves Lorenzo de'Medici from the Pazzi conspiracy.

1488
APPLE

14 SEPT 1485
FLYING MACHINE

1488
PROPHET

Formally inducted as an Assassin into the Brotherhood. Niccolò Machiavelli recognizes him as a Prophet.

Recovers the Apple brought back from Cyprus by the Templars.

Fails to save the Doge of Venice despite using Leonardo da Vinci's flying machine.

04 JUL 1488
THEFT

1491
COROMBO

Battle of Forlì. The Apple is stolen from Ezio by Girolamo Savonarola.

Travels to Spain and protects preparations for the expedition of Christoffa Corombo.

Liberates Florence from the influence of extremist monk Girolamo Savonarola and retrieves the Apple.

1497
LIBERATION

1500
DESTRUCTION

28 DEC 1499
MINERVA

1500
COPERNICUS

Protects Nicolaus Copernicus in his research.

Siege and destruction of Monteriggioni by Cesare Borgia who takes the Apple. Ezio hunts down the Borgias and their supporters in Rome.

Confrontation with Rodrigo Borgia who is now Pope. Meeting with Minerva in the Vatican Vault. She sends a message to Desmond via him.

1503
MENTOR

18 AUG 1503
APPLE

Machiavelli stands down as Mentor of the Brotherhood and gives the role to Ezio.

Retrieves the Apple hidden in St Peter's Basilica ahead of Cesare Borgia and uses it to eliminate the last of his support.

1503
FUTURE

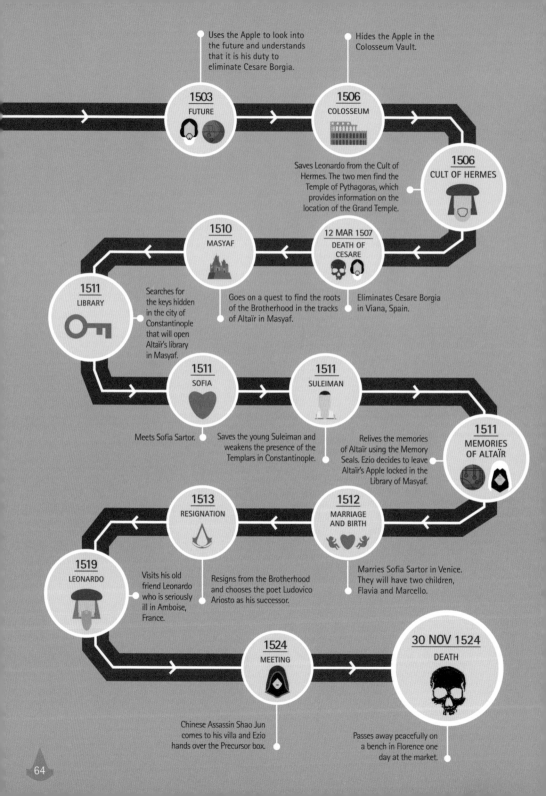

Uses the Apple to look into the future and understands that it is his duty to eliminate Cesare Borgia.

1506
COLOSSEUM

Hides the Apple in the Colosseum Vault.

1506
CULT OF HERMES

Saves Leonardo from the Cult of Hermes. The two men find the Temple of Pythagoras, which provides information on the location of the Grand Temple.

1510
MASYAF

12 MAR 1507
DEATH OF CESARE

1511
LIBRARY

Searches for the keys hidden in the city of Constantinople that will open Altaïr's library in Masyaf.

Goes on a quest to find the roots of the Brotherhood in the tracks of Altaïr in Masyaf.

Eliminates Cesare Borgia in Viana, Spain.

1511
SOFIA

1511
SULEIMAN

1511
MEMORIES OF ALTAÏR

Meets Sofia Sartor.

Saves the young Suleiman and weakens the presence of the Templars in Constantinople.

Relives the memories of Altaïr using the Memory Seals. Ezio decides to leave Altaïr's Apple locked in the Library of Masyaf.

1513
RESIGNATION

1512
MARRIAGE AND BIRTH

1519
LEONARDO

Visits his old friend Leonardo who is seriously ill in Amboise, France.

Resigns from the Brotherhood and chooses the poet Ludovico Ariosto as his successor.

Marries Sofia Sartor in Venice. They will have two children, Flavia and Marcello.

1524
MEETING

30 NOV 1524
DEATH

Chinese Assassin Shao Jun comes to his villa and Ezio hands over the Precursor box.

Passes away peacefully on a bench in Florence one day at the market.

"I HAVE LIVED MY LIFE AS BEST I COULD,
NOT KNOWING ITS PURPOSE, BUT DRAWN
FORWARD LIKE A MOTH TO A DISTANT
MOON; AND HERE AT LAST, I DISCOVER
A STRANGE TRUTH. THAT I AM ONLY A
CONDUIT FOR A MESSAGE THAT ELUDES
MY UNDERSTANDING."

1512

EDWARD KENWAY
THE ADVENTURER (1693-1735)

Edward is the ultimate adventurer. A privateer of the King of England turned pirate, he unwittingly becomes completely embroiled in the conflict between Templars and Assassins in the Caribbean. He switches from one camp to the other based purely on motives of personal gain. A founding member of the Pirate Republic of Nassau, he gradually realizes how empty his life is and joins the Assassins, for whom he will find the Observatory.

Born 10th March 1693 in Swansea, Wales

Parents: Bernard Kenway and Linette Kenway, farmers in Bristol

INFORMATION:

- Pirate blinded by the lure of riches until 1721

- Discovers the Observatory, numerous Temples, and a Shroud of Eden

- Father of Haytham Kenway, and grandfather of Ratonhnhaké:ton (Connor)

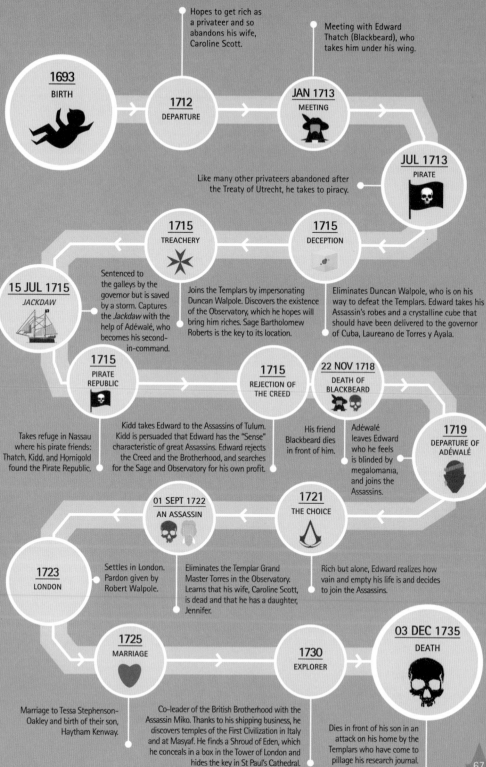

1693
BIRTH

1712
DEPARTURE

Hopes to get rich as a privateer and so abandons his wife, Caroline Scott.

JAN 1713
MEETING

Meeting with Edward Thatch (Blackbeard), who takes him under his wing.

JUL 1713
PIRATE

Like many other privateers abandoned after the Treaty of Utrecht, he takes to piracy.

1715
TREACHERY

1715
DECEPTION

Joins the Templars by impersonating Duncan Walpole. Discovers the existence of the Observatory, which he hopes will bring him riches. Sage Bartholomew Roberts is the key to its location.

Eliminates Duncan Walpole, who is on his way to defeat the Templars. Edward takes his Assassin's robes and a crystalline cube that should have been delivered to the governor of Cuba, Laureano de Torres y Ayala.

15 JUL 1715
JACKDAW

Sentenced to the galleys by the governor but is saved by a storm. Captures the *Jackdaw* with the help of Adéwalé, who becomes his second-in-command.

1715
PIRATE REPUBLIC

1715
REJECTION OF THE CREED

22 NOV 1718
DEATH OF BLACKBEARD

1719
DEPARTURE OF ADÉWALÉ

Takes refuge in Nassau where his pirate friends: Thatch, Kidd, and Hornigold found the Pirate Republic.

Kidd takes Edward to the Assassins of Tulum. Kidd is persuaded that Edward has the "Sense" characteristic of great Assassins. Edward rejects the Creed and the Brotherhood, and searches for the Sage and Observatory for his own profit.

His friend Blackbeard dies in front of him.

Adéwalé leaves Edward who he feels is blinded by megalomania, and joins the Assassins.

01 SEPT 1722
AN ASSASSIN

1721
THE CHOICE

1723
LONDON

Settles in London. Pardon given by Robert Walpole.

Eliminates the Templar Grand Master Torres in the Observatory. Learns that his wife, Caroline Scott, is dead and that he has a daughter, Jennifer.

Rich but alone, Edward realizes how vain and empty his life is and decides to join the Assassins.

1725
MARRIAGE

1730
EXPLORER

03 DEC 1735
DEATH

Marriage to Tessa Stephenson-Oakley and birth of their son, Haytham Kenway.

Co-leader of the British Brotherhood with the Assassin Miko. Thanks to his shipping business, he discovers temples of the First Civilization in Italy and at Masyaf. He finds a Shroud of Eden, which he conceals in a box in the Tower of London and hides the key in St Paul's Cathedral.

Dies in front of his son in an attack on his home by the Templars who have come to pillage his research journal.

HAYTHAM KENWAY
THE ARISTOCRAT (1725-1781)

Haytham Kenway is cold, calculating, charismatic, and expresses humor in the most unlikely situations. Marked by the death of his father and kidnapping of his half-sister, he finds an ideology in the Templars that matches his father's philosophy of questioning, and is a devout believer in the Order. He is tasked with searching for the Grand Temple and founding a local rite in the American colonies. Although he can imagine reconciliation between Assassins and Templars, he is fully convinced that the order and reason advocated by the Templars is the only future of humanity.

Born 4th December 1725 in London

Mother: Tessa Kenway (née Stephenson-Oakley)

Father: Former pirate Assassin Edward Kenway, who trains him from a very young age.

INFORMATION:

- Founder of the Templar Order's Colonial Rite

- Discovers the Grand Temple

- Wipes out almost all Assassins in the Great Purge

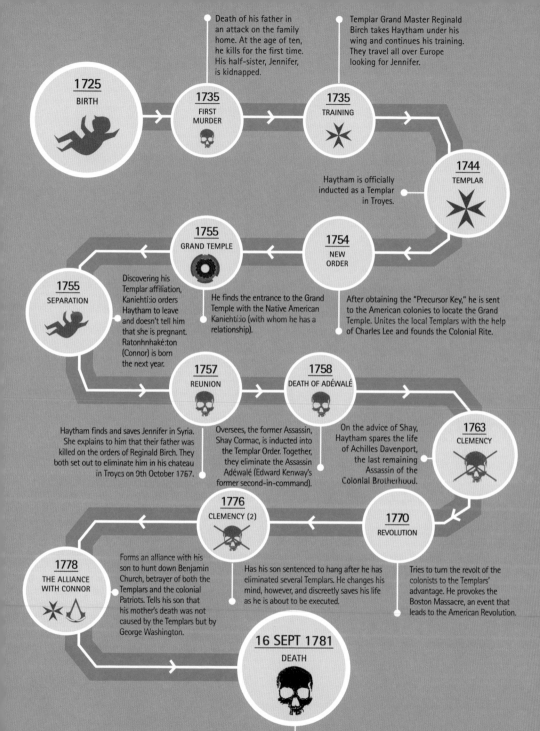

1725 BIRTH

1735 FIRST MURDER

Death of his father in an attack on the family home. At the age of ten, he kills for the first time. His half-sister, Jennifer, is kidnapped.

1735 TRAINING

Templar Grand Master Reginald Birch takes Haytham under his wing and continues his training. They travel all over Europe looking for Jennifer.

1744 TEMPLAR

Haytham is officially inducted as a Templar in Troyes.

1755 GRAND TEMPLE

He finds the entrance to the Grand Temple with the Native American Kaniehtí:io (with whom he has a relationship).

1754 NEW ORDER

After obtaining the "Precursor Key," he is sent to the American colonies to locate the Grand Temple. Unites the local Templars with the help of Charles Lee and founds the Colonial Rite.

1755 SEPARATION

Discovering his Templar affiliation, Kaniehtí:io orders Haytham to leave and doesn't tell him that she is pregnant. Ratonhnhaké:ton (Connor) is born the next year.

1757 REUNION

Haytham finds and saves Jennifer in Syria. She explains to him that their father was killed on the orders of Reginald Birch. They both set out to eliminate him in his chateau in Troyes on 9th October 1757.

1758 DEATH OF ADÉWALÉ

Oversees, the former Assassin, Shay Cormac, is inducted into the Templar Order. Together, they eliminate the Assassin Adéwalé (Edward Kenway's former second-in-command).

1763 CLEMENCY

On the advice of Shay, Haytham spares the life of Achilles Davenport, the last remaining Assassin of the Colonial Brotherhood.

1776 CLEMENCY (2)

Has his son sentenced to hang after he has eliminated several Templars. He changes his mind, however, and discreetly saves his life as he is about to be executed.

1770 REVOLUTION

Tries to turn the revolt of the colonists to the Templars' advantage. He provokes the Boston Massacre, an event that leads to the American Revolution.

1778 THE ALLIANCE WITH CONNOR

Forms an alliance with his son to hunt down Benjamin Church, betrayer of both the Templars and the colonial Patriots. Tells his son that his mother's death was not caused by the Templars but by George Washington.

16 SEPT 1781 DEATH

Final battle against his son at Fort George in New York. Haytham is fatally stabbed in the neck but feels a sense of pride in his son.

RATONHNHAKÉ:TON (CONNOR)
THE IDEALIST (1756-?)

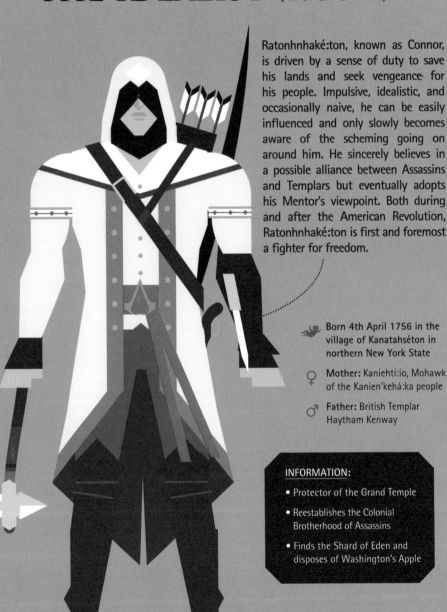

Ratonhnhaké:ton, known as Connor, is driven by a sense of duty to save his lands and seek vengeance for his people. Impulsive, idealistic, and occasionally naive, he can be easily influenced and only slowly becomes aware of the scheming going on around him. He sincerely believes in a possible alliance between Assassins and Templars but eventually adopts his Mentor's viewpoint. Both during and after the American Revolution, Ratonhnhaké:ton is first and foremost a fighter for freedom.

Born 4th April 1756 in the village of Kanatahséton in northern New York State

Mother: Kaniehtí:io, Mohawk of the Kanien'kehá:ka people

Father: British Templar Haytham Kenway

INFORMATION:

- Protector of the Grand Temple
- Reestablishes the Colonial Brotherhood of Assassins
- Finds the Shard of Eden and disposes of Washington's Apple

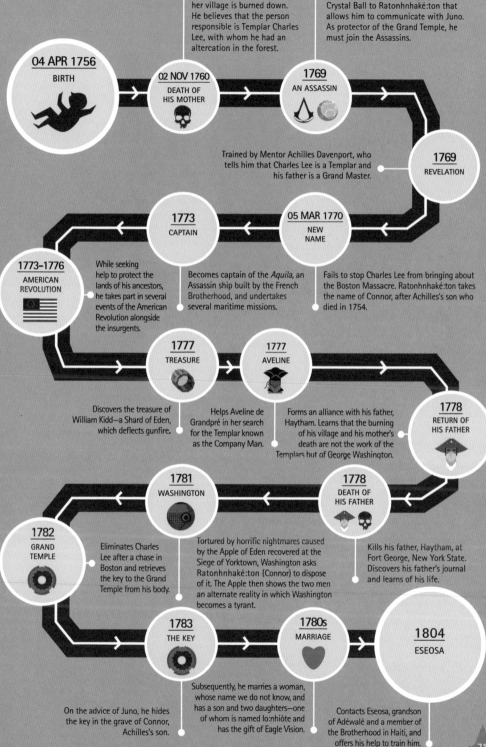

04 APR 1756
BIRTH

02 NOV 1760
DEATH OF
HIS MOTHER

Death of his mother when her village is burned down. He believes that the person responsible is Templar Charles Lee, with whom he had an altercation in the forest.

1769
AN ASSASSIN

The matriarch of the village gives a Crystal Ball to Ratonhnhaké:ton that allows him to communicate with Juno. As protector of the Grand Temple, he must join the Assassins.

1769
REVELATION

Trained by Mentor Achilles Davenport, who tells him that Charles Lee is a Templar and his father is a Grand Master.

1773
CAPTAIN

05 MAR 1770
NEW NAME

1773–1776
AMERICAN REVOLUTION

While seeking help to protect the lands of his ancestors, he takes part in several events of the American Revolution alongside the insurgents.

Becomes captain of the *Aquila*, an Assassin ship built by the French Brotherhood, and undertakes several maritime missions.

Fails to stop Charles Lee from bringing about the Boston Massacre. Ratonhnhaké:ton takes the name of Connor, after Achilles's son who died in 1754.

1777
TREASURE

1777
AVELINE

1778
RETURN OF HIS FATHER

Discovers the treasure of William Kidd—a Shard of Eden, which deflects gunfire.

Helps Aveline de Grandpré in her search for the Templar known as the Company Man.

Forms an alliance with his father, Haytham. Learns that the burning of his village and his mother's death are not the work of the Templars but of George Washington.

1781
WASHINGTON

1778
DEATH OF HIS FATHER

1782
GRAND TEMPLE

Eliminates Charles Lee after a chase in Boston and retrieves the key to the Grand Temple from his body.

Tortured by horrific nightmares caused by the Apple of Eden recovered at the Siege of Yorktown, Washington asks Ratonhnhaké:ton (Connor) to dispose of it. The Apple then shows the two men an alternate reality in which Washington becomes a tyrant.

Kills his father, Haytham, at Fort George, New York State. Discovers his father's journal and learns of his life.

1783
THE KEY

1780s
MARRIAGE

1804
ESEOSA

On the advice of Juno, he hides the key in the grave of Connor, Achilles's son.

Subsequently, he marries a woman, whose name we do not know, and has a son and two daughters—one of whom is named Io:nhiòte and has the gift of Eagle Vision.

Contacts Eseosa, grandson of Adéwalé and a member of the Brotherhood in Haiti, and offers his help to train him.

AVELINE DE GRANDPRÉ
THE LIBERATOR (1747-?)

An intrepid woman of character and a social chameleon, Aveline de Grandpré makes use of all her talents to fight slavery. As a result of her battles, she soon joins the Brotherhood but her relationship with her Mentor, Agaté, quickly becomes confrontational. She shares a taste for freedom with Ratonhnhaké:ton (Connor), who she meets in 1777. In dismantling a slave-trafficking operation, Aveline discovers the chamber of Chichen Itza in Mexico and the Prophecy Disk that tells of the rebellion of Adam and Eve.

Born 20th June 1747
in New Orleans

Mother: Jeanne, a slave

Father: Philippe de Grandpré,
a wealthy French merchant

INFORMATION:

- First playable female
  Assassin in the franchise.

- Mistress of disguise
  (lady, slave, or Assassin)

- Fights slavery
  and social injustice

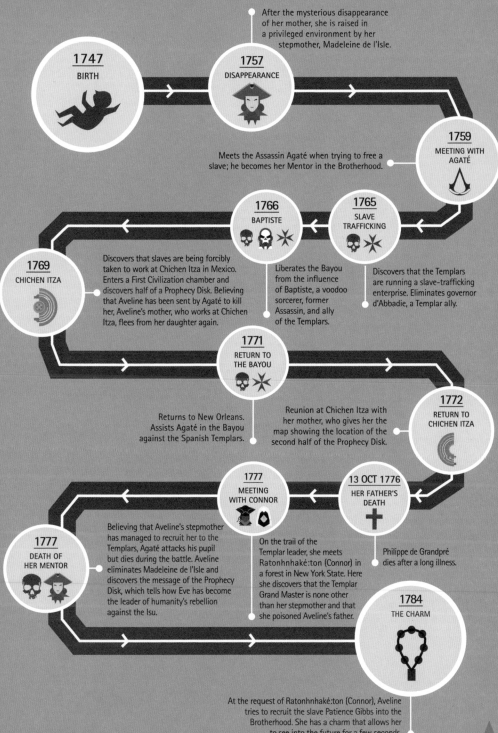

1747
BIRTH

1757
DISAPPEARANCE

After the mysterious disappearance of her mother, she is raised in a privileged environment by her stepmother, Madeleine de l'Isle.

1759
MEETING WITH AGATÉ

Meets the Assassin Agaté when trying to free a slave; he becomes her Mentor in the Brotherhood.

1766
BAPTISTE

1765
SLAVE TRAFFICKING

1769
CHICHEN ITZA

Discovers that slaves are being forcibly taken to work at Chichen Itza in Mexico. Enters a First Civilization chamber and discovers half of a Prophecy Disk. Believing that Aveline has been sent by Agaté to kill her, Aveline's mother, who works at Chichen Itza, flees from her daughter again.

Liberates the Bayou from the influence of Baptiste, a voodoo sorcerer, former Assassin, and ally of the Templars.

Discovers that the Templars are running a slave-trafficking enterprise. Eliminates governor d'Abbadie, a Templar ally.

1771
RETURN TO THE BAYOU

Returns to New Orleans. Assists Agaté in the Bayou against the Spanish Templars.

Reunion at Chichen Itza with her mother, who gives her the map showing the location of the second half of the Prophecy Disk.

1772
RETURN TO CHICHEN ITZA

1777
MEETING WITH CONNOR

13 OCT 1776
HER FATHER'S DEATH

1777
DEATH OF HER MENTOR

Believing that Aveline's stepmother has managed to recruit her to the Templars, Agaté attacks his pupil but dies during the battle. Aveline eliminates Madeleine de l'Isle and discovers the message of the Prophecy Disk, which tells how Eve has become the leader of humanity's rebellion against the Isu.

On the trail of the Templar leader, she meets Ratonhnhaké:ton (Connor) in a forest in New York State. Here she discovers that the Templar Grand Master is none other than her stepmother and that she poisoned Aveline's father.

Philippe de Grandpré dies after a long illness.

1784
THE CHARM

At the request of Ratonhnhaké:ton (Connor), Aveline tries to recruit the slave Patience Gibbs into the Brotherhood. She has a charm that allows her to see into the future for a few seconds.

73

ARNO DORIAN
THE ROMANTIC (1768-?)

A French–Austrian Assassin, Arno Dorian is a born romantic. Tormented by remorse and by his love for Élise, he is often driven by his impulses rather than wisdom. While rebel Templars try to manipulate the French Revolution, Arno starts upon a path of redemption.

Born 26th August 1768

Mother: Marie Dorian, an Austrian

Father: Charles Dorian, a French Assassin and member of the nobility living in Versailles

THE EIGHT TARGETS OF ARNO:

- **Charles Gabriel Sivert,** Templar, plotter against François de la Serre

- **Le Roi des Thunes,** assassin of de la Serre

- **Chrétien Lafrenière,** falsely accused of being responsible for the murder when in fact he had penned the letter warning of the plot

- **Frédéric Rouille,** Templar

- **Marie Lévesque,** Templar, plots to raise the price of grain

- **Louis-Michel le Peletier,** Templar, accomplice of Levésque, casts the final vote condemning Louis XVI to death

- **Aloys la Touche,** enforcer for le Roi des Thunes and an enthusiastic torturer

- **Maximilien de Robespierre,** politician in the pay of the Templars

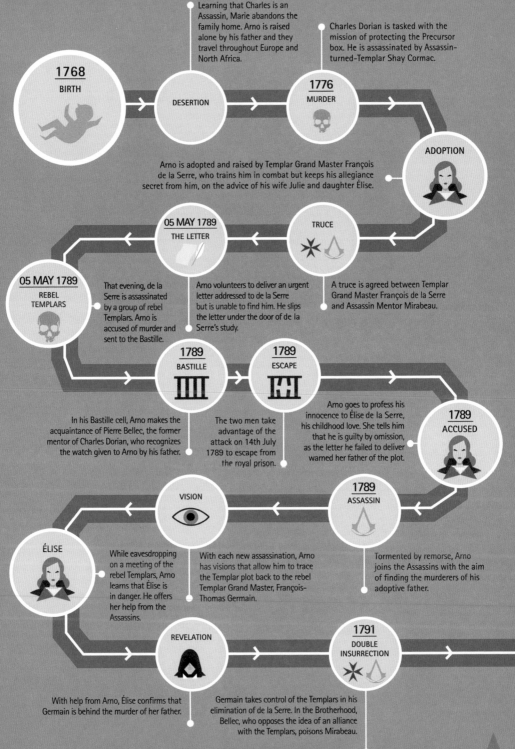

1768
BIRTH

DESERTION

Learning that Charles is an Assassin, Marie abandons the family home. Arno is raised alone by his father and they travel throughout Europe and North Africa.

1776
MURDER

Charles Dorian is tasked with the mission of protecting the Precursor box. He is assassinated by Assassin-turned-Templar Shay Cormac.

ADOPTION

Arno is adopted and raised by Templar Grand Master François de la Serre, who trains him in combat but keeps his allegiance secret from him, on the advice of his wife Julie and daughter Élise.

05 MAY 1789
THE LETTER

TRUCE

05 MAY 1789
REBEL TEMPLARS

That evening, de la Serre is assassinated by a group of rebel Templars. Arno is accused of murder and sent to the Bastille.

Arno volunteers to deliver an urgent letter addressed to de la Serre but is unable to find him. He slips the letter under the door of de la Serre's study.

A truce is agreed between Templar Grand Master François de la Serre and Assassin Mentor Mirabeau.

1789
BASTILLE

1789
ESCAPE

In his Bastille cell, Arno makes the acquaintance of Pierre Bellec, the former mentor of Charles Dorian, who recognizes the watch given to Arno by his father.

The two men take advantage of the attack on 14th July 1789 to escape from the royal prison.

1789
ACCUSED

Arno goes to profess his innocence to Élise de la Serre, his childhood love. She tells him that he is guilty by omission, as the letter he failed to deliver warned her father of the plot.

VISION

1789
ASSASSIN

ÉLISE

While eavesdropping on a meeting of the rebel Templars, Arno learns that Élise is in danger. He offers her help from the Assassins.

With each new assassination, Arno has visions that allow him to trace the Templar plot back to the rebel Templar Grand Master, François-Thomas Germain.

Tormented by remorse, Arno joins the Assassins with the aim of finding the murderers of his adoptive father.

REVELATION

1791
DOUBLE INSURRECTION

With help from Arno, Élise confirms that Germain is behind the murder of her father.

Germain takes control of the Templars in his elimination of de la Serre. In the Brotherhood, Bellec, who opposes the idea of an alliance with the Templars, poisons Mirabeau.

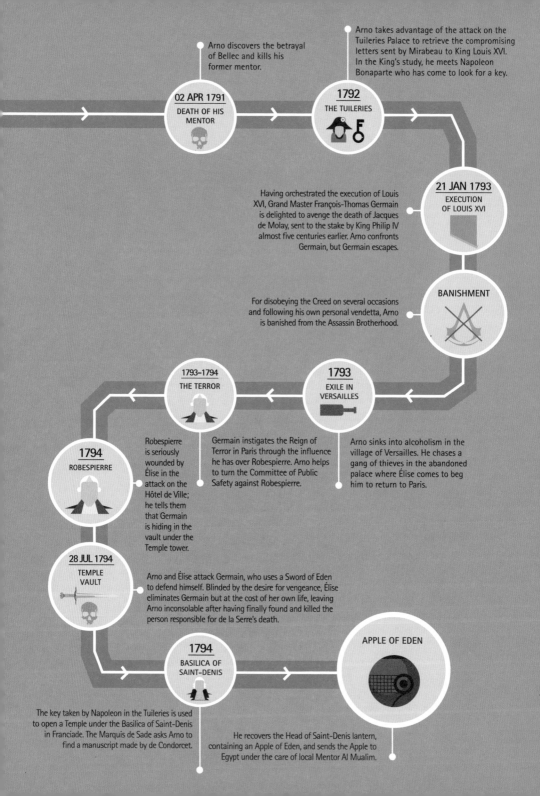

Arno discovers the betrayal of Bellec and kills his former mentor.

02 APR 1791
DEATH OF HIS MENTOR

Arno takes advantage of the attack on the Tuileries Palace to retrieve the compromising letters sent by Mirabeau to King Louis XVI. In the King's study, he meets Napoleon Bonaparte who has come to look for a key.

1792
THE TUILERIES

Having orchestrated the execution of Louis XVI, Grand Master François-Thomas Germain is delighted to avenge the death of Jacques de Molay, sent to the stake by King Philip IV almost five centuries earlier. Arno confronts Germain, but Germain escapes.

21 JAN 1793
EXECUTION OF LOUIS XVI

For disobeying the Creed on several occasions and following his own personal vendetta, Arno is banished from the Assassin Brotherhood.

BANISHMENT

1793–1794
THE TERROR

1793
EXILE IN VERSAILLES

Robespierre is seriously wounded by Élise in the attack on the Hôtel de Ville; he tells them that Germain is hiding in the vault under the Temple tower.

Germain instigates the Reign of Terror in Paris through the influence he has over Robespierre. Arno helps to turn the Committee of Public Safety against Robespierre.

Arno sinks into alcoholism in the village of Versailles. He chases a gang of thieves in the abandoned palace where Élise comes to beg him to return to Paris.

1794
ROBESPIERRE

28 JUL 1794
TEMPLE VAULT

Arno and Élise attack Germain, who uses a Sword of Eden to defend himself. Blinded by the desire for vengeance, Élise eliminates Germain but at the cost of her own life, leaving Arno inconsolable after having finally found and killed the person responsible for de la Serre's death.

APPLE OF EDEN

1794
BASILICA OF SAINT-DENIS

The key taken by Napoleon in the Tuileries is used to open a Temple under the Basilica of Saint-Denis in Franciade. The Marquis de Sade asks Arno to find a manuscript made by de Condorcet.

He recovers the Head of Saint-Denis lantern, containing an Apple of Eden, and sends the Apple to Egypt under the care of local Mentor Al Mualim.

"THE CREED OF THE ASSASSIN
BROTHERHOOD TEACHES US THAT
NOTHING IS FORBIDDEN TO US. ONCE, I
THOUGHT THAT MEANT WE WERE FREE TO
DO AS WE WOULD. TO PURSUE OUR IDEALS,
NO MATTER THE COST. I UNDERSTAND
NOW. NOT A GRANT OF PERMISSION. THE
CREED IS A WARNING."

1794

EVIE FRYE
THE INTELLECTUAL (1847-?)

Twins Evie and Jacob Frye are very different but well matched. The older twin by four minutes, Evie is fascinated by the First Civilization and has great respect for the Creed. As for her younger twin, Jacob rarely thinks about the consequences of his actions, which are often

Born 9th November 1847

♀ Mother: Cecily Frye, member of the British Brotherhood of Assassins. Dies in childbirth

INFORMATION:

- Thoughtful intellectual
- Discovers a Precursor necklace and Shroud of Eden

BIRTH

JACOB FRYE
THE BANDIT (1847-?)

spontaneous and aggressive. After the death of their father, they decide to liberate London, which has been in the grip of oppressive Templar rule since the death of Edward Kenway. They are knighted by Queen Victoria for saving her life.

♂ **Father:** Ethan Frye, member of the British Brotherhood of Assassins.

They are raised by their grandmother, and then by their father in Crawley, a town in South East England, when he returns from India.

INFORMATION:

- Impulsive and aggressive with megalomaniac tendencies
- Rebuilds the London Brotherhood

1847

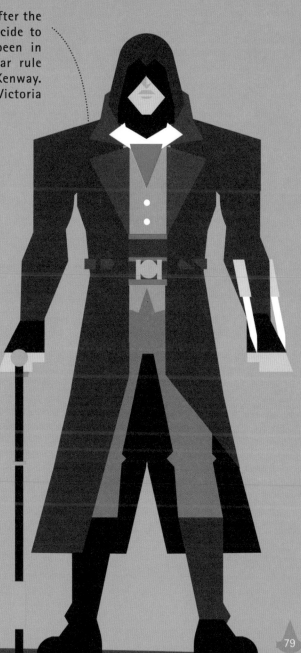

Ethan Frye returns from exile and trains
his children to become Assassins.

1853
RETURN OF THEIR FATHER

1868
ARRIVAL IN LONDON

Ethan Frye dies of natural causes. The twins
leave Crawley to liberate London
from the Templars.

1868
SHROUD OF EDEN

Evie saves Henry Green and
finds leads to the Shroud of Eden
hidden under Buckingham Palace.

Jacob eliminates the Templars working
for Starrick. He also saves the life of
Prime Minister Benjamin Disraeli. He
joins forces with Maxwell Roth, leader
of the enemy gang, to weaken
Starrick, but then eliminates
him because of Roth's mania
for killing.

1868
STARRICK

Together with Henry Green, the
twins eliminate Crawford Starrick
in the Buckingham Palace Vault
and retrieve the Shroud of Eden.

1868
GANG WARFARE

Jacob, Evie, and Henry Green are knighted by
Queen Victoria for preventing Starrick from
assassinating her.

1868
KNIGHTED

Evie and Henry get
married and relocate
to India. They live
there for around
20 years.

1873
INDIA

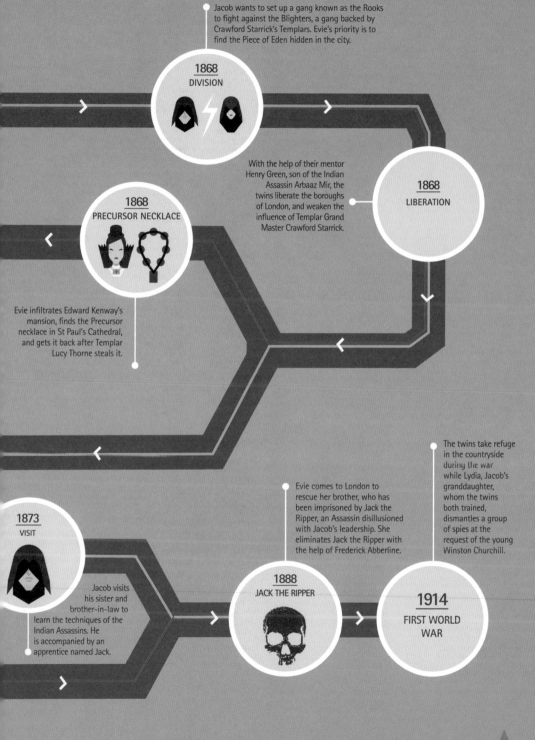

Jacob wants to set up a gang known as the Rooks to fight against the Blighters, a gang backed by Crawford Starrick's Templars. Evie's priority is to find the Piece of Eden hidden in the city.

1868
DIVISION

With the help of their mentor Henry Green, son of the Indian Assassin Arbaaz Mir, the twins liberate the boroughs of London, and weaken the influence of Templar Grand Master Crawford Starrick.

1868
LIBERATION

1868
PRECURSOR NECKLACE

Evie infiltrates Edward Kenway's mansion, finds the Precursor necklace in St Paul's Cathedral, and gets it back after Templar Lucy Thorne steals it.

The twins take refuge in the countryside during the war while Lydia, Jacob's granddaughter, whom the twins both trained, dismantles a group of spies at the request of the young Winston Churchill.

1873
VISIT

Jacob visits his sister and brother-in-law to learn the techniques of the Indian Assassins. He is accompanied by an apprentice named Jack.

Evie comes to London to rescue her brother, who has been imprisoned by Jack the Ripper, an Assassin disillusioned with Jacob's leadership. She eliminates Jack the Ripper with the help of Frederick Abberline.

1888
JACK THE RIPPER

1914
FIRST WORLD WAR

BAYEK
THE ORIGIN (DATES OF BIRTH AND DEATH UNKNOWN)

The last of the Medjay, and protector of Cleopatra, Bayek travels the Egyptian deserts in the period of the last pharaohs. With Aya his wife, he creates the organization of the "Hidden Ones," the beginnings of the Assassin Brotherhood.

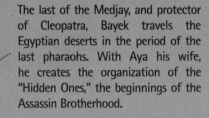
Born in Siwa, an Egyptian oasis on the Libyan border.

♀ Mother: Ahmose

♂ Father: Sabu, a Medjay protector of the region

INFORMATION:

- Bayek's enemies, the Order of the Ancients, also known as the Snake, form the beginnings of the Templar Order

- He is accompanied by Senu, a Bonelli's eagle

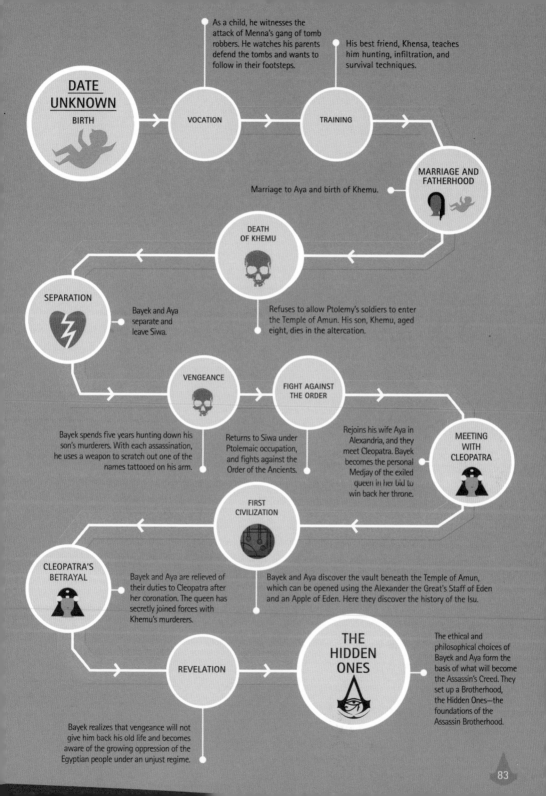

DATE UNKNOWN
BIRTH

VOCATION

As a child, he witnesses the attack of Menna's gang of tomb robbers. He watches his parents defend the tombs and wants to follow in their footsteps.

TRAINING

His best friend, Khensa, teaches him hunting, infiltration, and survival techniques.

MARRIAGE AND FATHERHOOD

Marriage to Aya and birth of Khemu.

DEATH OF KHEMU

SEPARATION

Bayek and Aya separate and leave Siwa.

Refuses to allow Ptolemy's soldiers to enter the Temple of Amun. His son, Khemu, aged eight, dies in the altercation.

VENGEANCE

FIGHT AGAINST THE ORDER

Bayek spends five years hunting down his son's murderers. With each assassination, he uses a weapon to scratch out one of the names tattooed on his arm.

Returns to Siwa under Ptolemaic occupation, and fights against the Order of the Ancients.

Rejoins his wife Aya in Alexandria, and they meet Cleopatra. Bayek becomes the personal Medjay of the exiled queen in her bid to win back her throne.

MEETING WITH CLEOPATRA

FIRST CIVILIZATION

CLEOPATRA'S BETRAYAL

Bayek and Aya are relieved of their duties to Cleopatra after her coronation. The queen has secretly joined forces with Khemu's murderers.

Bayek and Aya discover the vault beneath the Temple of Amun, which can be opened using the Alexander the Great's Staff of Eden and an Apple of Eden. Here they discover the history of the Isu.

THE HIDDEN ONES

The ethical and philosophical choices of Bayek and Aya form the basis of what will become the Assassin's Creed. They set up a Brotherhood, the Hidden Ones—the foundations of the Assassin Brotherhood.

REVELATION

Bayek realizes that vengeance will not give him back his old life and becomes aware of the growing oppression of the Egyptian people under an unjust regime.

ASSASSINS' HQ

Each Assassin sets out on missions from his or her own base. This can be the headquarters of the local Brotherhood but other characters have made stranger choices . . .

ORIGINAL

CLASSIC

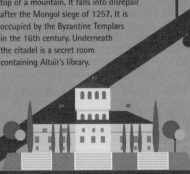

RATONHNHAKÉ:TON (CONNOR)
lives in the manor on the Davenport Homestead. Achilles Davenport passes on the manor and lands to Ratonhnhaké:ton (Connor), who develops an entire community there. He hides the key to the Grand Temple in the graveyard on the property.

ALTAÏR IBN-LA'AHAD
is based in the citadel of Masyaf (in what is now Syria). A historic Brotherhood fortress perched at the top of a mountain. It falls into disrepair after the Mongol siege of 1257. It is occupied by the Byzantine Templars in the 16th century. Underneath the citadel is a secret room containing Altaïr's library.

EZIO AUDITORE
lives in a villa in Monteriggioni (Tuscany, Italy), home to the Auditore family since 1321. It contains secret underground chambers and a family crypt. It is all but destroyed and abandoned after the siege led by Cesare Borgia on 2nd January 1500. It is subsequently reoccupied in 2012 by a group of Assassins.

AVELINE DE GRANDPRÉ
sets up her HQ in a warehouse in the docks of New Orleans. Assisted by Gérald Blanc, Aveline conducts her investigations.

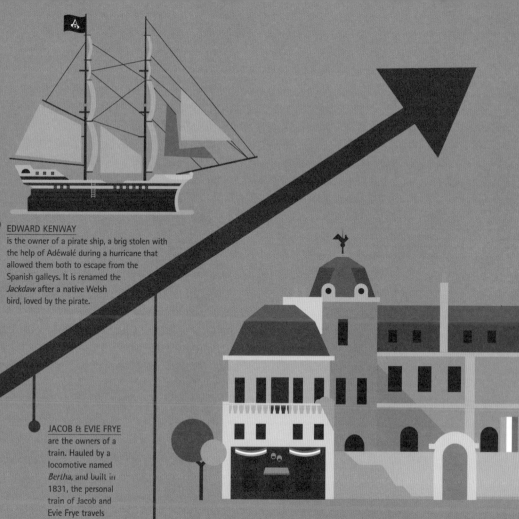

EDWARD KENWAY
is the owner of a pirate ship, a brig stolen with the help of Adéwalé during a hurricane that allowed them both to escape from the Spanish galleys. It is renamed the *Jackdaw* after a native Welsh bird, loved by the pirate.

JACOB & EVIE FRYE
are the owners of a train. Hauled by a locomotive named *Bertha*, and built in 1831, the personal train of Jacob and Evie Frye travels around London and is guarded by the faithful Agnes.

ARNO DORIAN
is the owner of the Café Théâtre. Gradually renovated as he completes his missions in Paris, Arno Dorian's Café Théâtre is located in the heart of the Île Saint-Louis opposite Notre-Dame Cathedral. It is a place to watch plays and seek the latest information on the French Revolution.

THE SCARS

Certain characters bear the same scars on their faces—some are there from birth as a sign of shared history and memory, while others simply tell of their adventures.

EDWARD   CONNOR

ALTAÏR   EZIO

AVELINE   DESMOND

+ *

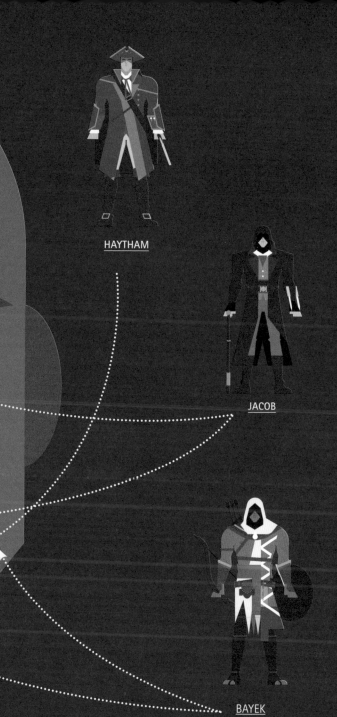

HAYTHAM

JACOB

BAYEK

CHAPTER 4
BEHIND THE SCENES OF THE FRANCHISE

FRANCHISE

ANTIQUITY

Although they are not yet called Assassins and Templars, there are two groups that exist with conflicting ideologies. Bayek and Aya work for the freedom of the Egyptian people and fight against Caesar and Cleopatra's authoritarian policies.

ASSASSIN'S CREED ORIGINS  PS4, PS4 Pro, XBOX One X

(1) (1)

	PC		SHORT FILM
CONSOLE		FACEBOOK GAME
MOBILE GAME		MANGA
NOVEL		COMICS

Legend icons:
- PC
- CONSOLE
- MOBILE GAME
- NOVEL
- SHORT FILM
- FACEBOOK GAME
- MANGA
- COMICS

MIDDLE AGES: THE FOUNDATIONS OF ALTAÏR

Although he is not responsible for the founding of the Assassin Brotherhood, it is Altaïr who reestablishes it. He eliminates the traitor Al Mualim, studies an Apple of Eden, improves the Hidden Blade, and reforms the Creed.

ASSASSIN'S CREED 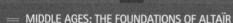 Xbox 360, PS3

(1) (1) (2)

RENAISSANCE: THE EZIO COLLECTION

 Xbox One, PS4

Initially driven by personal vendetta, Ezio Auditore quickly becomes the Mentor of the Brotherhood and disseminates the ideas of the Renaissance throughout Europe and as far as Constantinople.

ASSASSIN'S CREED II  Xbox 360, PS3

ASSASSIN'S CREED BROTHERHOOD — Xbox 360, PS3

ASSASSIN'S CREED REVELATIONS — Xbox 360, PS3

(3) (2) (1) (3)

THE AMERICAN SAGA

More than three generations of the Kenway family make their mark in the 18th century. The first to distinguish himself is a pirate who scours the Caribbean and coasts of Africa before becoming an Assassin Mentor in London. His son is one of the most important Templar Grand Masters active in the American Revolution; and his child in turn is tormented by the conflict between his roots and the heritage his father wanted to pass on to him.

ASSASSIN'S CREED III — PS3, Xbox 360, WiiU

ASSASSIN'S CREED III LIBERATION — PS Vita, then port to PS3, Xbox 360

ASSASSIN'S CREED IV BLACK FLAG — PS3, PS4, Xbox 360, Xbox One, Wii U

(1)

ASSASSIN'S CREED IV: FREEDOM CRY

ASSASSIN'S CREED ROGUE — PS3, PS4, PS4 Pro, Xbox 360, Xbox One, Xbox One X

Black Flag DLC available as standalone on PS3 and PS4

(2) (1)

OVERVIEW

FRENCH REVOLUTION

The Templars manipulate the Revolution as they seek vengeance against King Louis XVI for the death of Jacques de Molay. They attempt to instigate the Terror as a means of subjugating the population. An alliance and love story forms between Assassin Arno Dorian and Templar heiress Élise de la Serre.

ASSASSIN'S CREED UNITY 🖥️ 🎮 PS4, Xbox One (1)

IMPERIAL CHINA

A former concubine of the Zhengde Emperor, Assassin Shao Jun goes to get advice from Ezio Auditore in Florence, before returning to China to seek vengeance and rebuild the local Brotherhood.

ASSASSIN'S CREED CHRONICLES: CHINA 🖥️ 🎮 PS4, Xbox One, PS Vita (1) ▶️

SIKH EMPIRE

On the eve of British colonization, Assassin Arbaaz Mir is tasked with protecting Maharaja Ranjit Singh, guardian of the Koh-i-Noor—the largest diamond in the world, which is actually a powerful First Civilization artifact.

ASSASSIN'S CREED CHRONICLES: INDIA 🖥️ 🎮 PS4, Xbox One, PS Vita (1)

VICTORIAN ERA

Twins Jacob and Evie Frye regain control of London—capital of the largest colonial empire in the world—from the hands of Crawford Starrick, a ruthless businessman and Templar Grand Master.

ASSASSIN'S CREED SYNDICATE 🖥️ 🎮 PS4, Xbox One (1) (1)

RUSSIAN REVOLUTION

In 1918 Assassin Nikolaï Orelov has to retrieve an artifact from the Bolsheviks who are holding the Tsar and his family hostage.

ASSASSIN'S CREED CHRONICLES: RUSSIA 🖥️ 🎮 PS4, Xbox One, PS Vita (2)

A BIT OF GEOGRAPHY

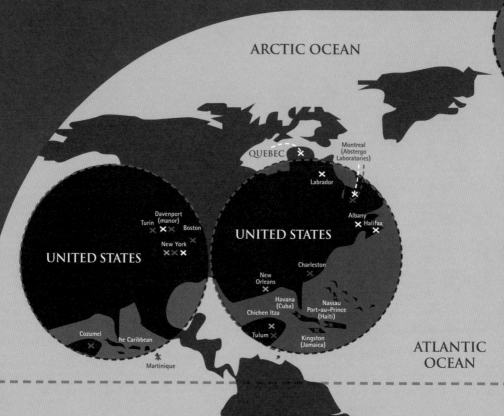

ARCTIC OCEAN

QUEBEC

Montreal
(Abstergo
Laboratories)

Labrador

Davenport
(manor)
Turin   Boston

UNITED STATES   UNITED STATES

Albany
Halifax

New York

Charleston

New
Orleans

Havana
(Cuba)
Chichen Itza   Nassau
Port-au-Prince
(Haiti)
Cozumel
The Caribbean   Tulum   Kingston
(Jamaica)

ATLANTIC
OCEAN

Martinique

PACIFIC
OCEAN

BRAZIL

N

W   E

S

ANTARCTIC

The *Assassin's Creed* series is an opportunity to revise not only history but also geography. Over the games, players get to travel the world.

UNITED KINGDOM

Croydon
✕ London

✕ Saint-Denis
✕ ✕ Paris
Versailles

FRANCE

Constantinople

TURKEY

✕ Cappadocia

Venice
✕

Florence
✕ Forlì ✕
Monteriggioni ✕

San ✕
Gimignano

ITALY

Rome ✕ ✕ Rome
(Abstergo (Vatican)
Laboratories)

✕ Masyaf (fortress)

Acre ✕
Arsuf ✕ ✕ Damas
✕ Jerusalem
(Solomon's
Temple)

MIDDLE EAST

✕ Viana
✕ Lisbon

INDIAN OCEAN

✕ ASSASSIN'S CREED

✕ ASSASSIN'S CREED
THE EZIO COLLECTION

✕ ASSASSIN'S CREED UNITY

✕ ASSASSIN'S CREED SYNDICATE

✕ ASSASSIN'S CREED III

✕ ASSASSIN'S CREED IV BLACK FLAG

✕ ASSASSIN'S CREED ROGUE

✕ ASSASSIN'S CREED LIBERATION

OCEAN

UBISOFT STUDIOS AROUND THE WORLD

QUEBEC STUDIO (CANADA)

Leonardo da Vinci's machines
Finding the Masyaf Keys
The Davenport Homestead, Sewers,
Eagle Flight, and Tyranny of King
Washington DLC
Freedom Cry DLC
Lead studio on

Quebec

Toronto

Montreal

QUEBEC STUDIO, CANADA

MONTREAL STUDIO, CANADA

TORONTO (CANADA)

Co-development on
The studio designed the
part of Paris south of
the Seine.

ATLANTIC
OCEAN

LEAD STUDIOS

SUPPORT STUDIOS

AC

AC IV Black Flag

AC II

AC Rogue

AC Brotherhood

AC Unity

AC Revelations

AC Syndicate

AC III

AC Origins

To produce each game, the work of several development studios around the world has to be coordinated. While Montreal is usually the lead studio, bits of the *Assassin's Creed* series have been crafted all over the planet.

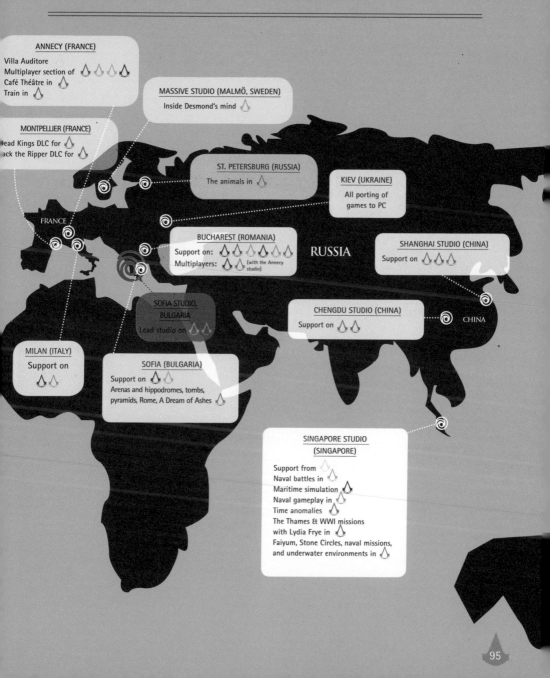

ANNECY (FRANCE)
Villa Auditore
Multiplayer section of
Café Théâtre in
Train in

MASSIVE STUDIO (MALMÖ, SWEDEN)
Inside Desmond's mind

MONTPELLIER (FRANCE)
ead Kings DLC for
ack the Ripper DLC for

ST. PETERSBURG (RUSSIA)
The animals in

KIEV (UKRAINE)
All porting of
games to PC

FRANCE

BUCHAREST (ROMANIA)
Support on:
Multiplayers: (with the Annecy studio)

RUSSIA

SHANGHAI STUDIO (CHINA)
Support on

SOFIA STUDIO, BULGARIA
Lead studio on

CHENGDU STUDIO (CHINA)
Support on

CHINA

MILAN (ITALY)
Support on

SOFIA (BULGARIA)
Support on
Arenas and hippodromes, tombs,
pyramids, Rome, A Dream of Ashes

SINGAPORE STUDIO (SINGAPORE)
Support from
Naval battles in
Maritime simulation
Naval gameplay in
Time anomalies
The Thames & WWI missions
with Lydia Frye in
Faiyum, Stone Circles, naval missions,
and underwater environments in

In the Davenport Homestead, Connor can feed a turkey after whistling for it. It will follow him everywhere. If the player enters the "Konami Code" (for Xbox: up, up, down, down, left, right, left, right, B, A; for Playstation: up, up, down, down, left, right, left, right, circle, cross; for PC: 2, 2, 4, 4, 1, 3, 1, 3, E, space), an Assassin hood will appear on the turkey's head.

ACKNOWLEDGMENTS

Many thanks to Justine Villeneuve, Étienne Bouvier, Clémence Deleuze, Pauline de Gourcuff, Gabrielle Lévy Delaveau, and the Ubisoft France teams. Many thanks to Aymar Azaizïa, Anouk Bachman, Antoine Ceszynski (for his Eagle Vision!), and the Ubisoft Montreal teams.

Thank you to the Assassin's Creed community and especially all those around the world who have contributed to the assassinscreed.wikia.com wiki!

Guillaume Delalande would like to thank his editors, Jean-Baptiste Roux and Antoine Béon; Emmanuel Carré and Pascal Lecointe at Ubisoft; and, on a more personal note, Julien, Kevin, Yohann, and Julien Baptist for their support on this project.